Creating Your Perfect Family Size

Creating Your Perfect Family Size

How to Make an Informed Decision About Having a Baby

Alan M. Singer, PhD

JOSSEY-BASS
A Wiley Imprint
www.josseybass.com

Published by Jossey-Bass
A Wiley Imprint
989 Market Street, San Francisco, CA 94103-1741—www.josseybass.com

The contents of this work are intended to further general scientific research, understanding, and discussion only and are not intended and should not be relied upon as recommending or promoting a specific method, diagnosis, or treatment by physicians for any particular patient. The publisher and the author make no representations or warranties with respect to the accuracy or completeness of the contents of this work and specifically disclaim all warranties, including without limitation any implied warranties of fitness for a particular purpose. In view of ongoing research, equipment modifications, changes in governmental regulations, and the constant flow of information relating to the use of medicines, equipment, and devices, the reader is urged to review and evaluate the information provided in the package insert or instructions for each medicine, equipment, or device for, among other things, any changes in the instructions or indication of usage and for added warnings and precautions. Readers should consult with a specialist where appropriate. The fact that an organization or Web site is referred to in this work as a citation and/or a potential source of further information does not mean that the author or the publisher endorses the information that the organization or Web site may provide or recommendations it may make. Further, readers should be aware that Internet Web sites listed in this work may have changed or disappeared between when this work was written and when it is read. No warranty may be created or extended by any promotional statements for this work. Neither the publisher nor the author shall be liable for any damages arising herefrom.

Jossey-Bass books and products are available through most bookstores. To contact Jossey-Bass directly call our Customer Care Department within the U.S. at 800-956-7739, outside the U.S. at 317-572-3986, or fax 317-572-4002.

Jossey-Bass also publishes its books in a variety of electronic formats. Some content that appears in print may not be available in electronic books.

Library of Congress Cataloging-in-Publication Data

Singer, Alan M., date.
    Creating your perfect family size: how to make an informed decision about having a baby/Alan M. Singer.
        p.   cm.
    Includes bibliographical references and index.
    ISBN 978-0-470-90031-4 (pbk.); ISBN 978-1-118-02551-2 (ebk);
    ISBN 978-1-118-02552-9 (ebk); 978-1-118-02553-6 (ebk)
        1. Family size—Decision making.   2. Family planning—Decision making.
3. Birth intervals.   I. Title.
    HQ760.S56   2011
    363.9'6—dc22

                                                          2010053642

Printed in the United States of America
FIRST EDITION
PB Printing   10 9 8 7 6 5 4 3 2 1

To my parents (of blessed memory), Rita Rose and
Joseph Singer, who are my role models for parenting.
To my wife, Shanie, of thirty-three years.
And to our children, Menucha and Noach, Noam and Racheli,
Yedida, and Zahava, who are my inspirations for this book.
You taught me how to be a good father.

Contents

Acknowledgments

Kenny Miller: The contrarian who battles pessimism with humor, and triumphs.

Ronnie Katz: A *connector* whose response to a friend in need is to put all of his resources at your disposal.

Marc Singer: My brother the finance wiz, who helped me formulate the financial impact of decisions about family size.

Rhea Basroon: No person I know has more creative ideas and solutions for getting the job done.

Noach Wolfe: My son-in-law, who convinced me and guided me into the world of social media.

Shiri Alyssa: A *deepest depths* friend who gives support and advice with brazen candor.

Ruben Gotlieb: A friend whose speed in assisting is exceeded only by his black-belt roundhouse kick.

Rabbi Eugene and Dr. Annette Labovitz: The team that launched my spiritual quest, which led to my marriage and children. Thank you for sharing your home and your inspiration.

Dan Benson: A friend who, when asked for a favor, first responds *yes* and then asks what is needed.

Harry Glazer: Literary peer, author, friend, and maven.

Bruce Arbit: The visionary of Milwaukee.

Professor Yetta Appel (of blessed memory): She singlehandedly rescued me from the label "all but dissertation" and showed me how carefully one must draw conclusions from one's data.

Paulina Dennis: For her years of edits, suggestions, and interpretative comments on this manuscript.

The couples: To the multitude of couples who shared their deeply personal stories that are the case histories that form the foundation of this book.

To the parents of children with special needs: You are my heroes!

Mark W. Smith: Author, attorney, and master of the fine print.

Stacey Glick (Dystel and Goderich): As my favorite literary agent, you are a true professional and steadfast guiding light.

The production staff at Jossey-Bass: My thanks to Nana Twumasi, Carol Hartland, Michele Jones, Francie Jones, Sylvia Coates, Sophia Ho, and Joanne Farness, who worked hard to take this book to the finish line.

Alan Rinzler: My editor at Jossey-Bass receives special thanks for his wise input and enthusiastic belief in this project from day one.

Naomi Lucks: Last, but certainly not least, the *word sculptor extraordinaire* who whipped this book into shape.

I sincerely thank you all.

Creating Your
Perfect Family Size

Introduction

When I was a boy, my father used to say, "When all else fails, read the directions." I wish I could recommend that approach for deciding whether or not parents should have another child. But unlike appliances, marriages and families do not come with instruction manuals! Personally, having children has always been a blessing for my wife and me, as we found out with each of our four, and now with our grandchildren.

And that's fine for me. But . . . how the heck do *you* figure out how many children to have? How many children should there be in a "perfect" family? Should you have one, two, three, more? Do you really need to balance boys and girls? What's the optimum interval between children? And how do you know when to say "enough"?

The good news is that there is no one-size-fits-all family—there is only the family that fits you and your partner, and whose size you agree on together, one child at a time. This book will give you and your partner insights and information about how to make these crucial decisions, toward the goal of enabling you to have a thriving marriage with children.

Making the Decision That's Right for You

Today we encounter families whose descriptions are far different from what was thought to be the norm. Blended families, couples first having children in their forties, and single parents are all commonplace. Often we can't help but wonder which families are the happiest and which are the healthiest. This book will take you step-by-step through the issues that concern you most as you make your decisions about family size.

We'll look at the commonly cited advantages and disadvantages of having families of different sizes, descriptions of the lifestyles of different size families, and the latest research on family size to date. We'll also hear stories of the experiences of a wide variety of couples and their decisions about family size. Most important, you'll get a chance to explore your own thinking and perhaps question some thoughts about family well-being you didn't even know you had.

How the Book Works

The core of *Creating Your Perfect Family Size* is a series of comprehensive self-assessment quizzes, which you will find at the end of every chapter. Topics range from issues of physical health, mental health, and work-related stresses to financial situations and obligations and marital success and happiness.

The self-assessments are designed to help you determine what your family can handle based on personal needs, financial pressures, the health of your relationship, and the goals of any family. Their purpose is to inspire meaningful conversation and insight between you and your partner. There are no right or wrong responses; there is only *your* response and your partner's response. (You'll also find the self-assessments gathered together in one section following the Epilogue. Although it will be tempting to turn right to the self-assessments, I hope you will take time to read each chapter first!)

This book is intended for readers in a variety of situations. Perhaps you instinctively want a child, or you always planned on having a family, or you suddenly decided to have a child after watching your siblings, friends, or other parents with children. Perhaps you already know that you want to have a child—or add another child to your family—as you begin to read this book. And that's all good.

During my entire professional career spanning more than three decades, I have never encouraged a couple to have a child. Having a child does not repair problematic marriages and does not increase marital satisfaction. The desire to have a child must be deep rooted and overwhelming. It is not a matter of keeping up with the Joneses.

Each child is a unique and precious gift. Your care of each child is an awesome responsibility. Use the insights and information you get from this book to determine when to start a family, when to add to your family, and what the optimum number of children is for your specific lifestyle. Whether you decide to have just one child or a houseful, that's up to you. Think about whether this is the ideal time for your family to grow in size, rather than what the "ideal family size" is or the number of children you "always wanted." This thoughtful approach will help you enjoy the best quality of well-being for you, your partner, and your family, no matter the size.

Above all, talk to your partner, use the questions in the book to clarify your own feelings, consider your responsibilities and resources, then do what's right for you.

ALAN SINGER
Spring 2011

Why Do You Want to Have Children?

> How can you love so much someone who drives you
> so crazy and makes such constant demands? How
> can you devote yourself to a vocation in which you
> are certain to be made peripheral, if not redundant?
> How can we joyfully embrace the notion that we
> have ceased to be the center of our own universe?
> —Anna Quindlen[1]

Here's something most parents would agree on: the child sleeping on your shoulder is worth about a billion bucks. Despite the late nights, sleep deprivation, stress, strained family finances, lack of balance between work and home, and other unwanted pressures unique to you only, each developmental step—first words, first steps, first book read—is more inspiring and fascinating than the previous one.

It's like falling in love. Parents become enthralled with their children's accomplishments, their tiniest expressions, and the love they give parents in return. Raising a family isn't always easy, but most of us come to feel that it's worth whatever time or money or dreams we gave up to make it possible. In short, we can't remember what life was like before parenthood—and some of us even want to become parents again and again.

Simple and powerful as these motivations are, we make the decision to have a child, to stop having children, or to add to the family for all sorts of conscious and unconscious reasons—emotional, psychological, financial, pragmatic, even spiritual. Sometimes these reasons clash with our real needs, of which we may be unaware.

For most of us, parenthood doesn't quite work out as we had envisioned. Most of the time, that's because we base our dream of the perfect family on unexplored motivations and experiences that come into focus only after our children are born.

I'm assuming that you're reading this book to learn how you can choose the perfect family size for you and your partner. Underneath all the various issues we will address in the rest of this book—timing, small families versus large families, cultural and religious issues, special needs and blended families—is one fundamental question: Why do *you* want to have children in the first place? The desire to be a parent is not universal and automatic, so . . . what's *your* reason?

REALITY CHECK
How Much Does It Cost to Raise a Child?

Hal is a thirty-eight-year-old software engineer married to Kristen, a thirty-nine-year-old graphic designer. They have been married for six years, live in Center City, Philadelphia, and have one child, a three-year-old daughter. When the recession hit, they found themselves struggling financially. Reluctantly, but after much discussion and soul searching, they've decided to stop at one child—for now, at least. Kristin explains, "If we were better off financially, it wouldn't even be a question."

It costs a lot of money to provide our children with food, cloth-ing, education, and adequate health care for two decades—or more, if a graduate degree is required. According to the U.S. Department of Agriculture's 2009 annual report, the average middle-income, two-parent family can expect to spend from $11,650 to $13,530 per year, depending on the age of the child.[2] And with private educa-tion and top-level health care, that amount can be a lot more.

When you and your partner are contemplating an increase in family size, you need to consider both *direct and indirect costs*. Direct costs related to children include housing, food, education, clothing, and medical care. Housing is an important consideration as your family size grows and you need more room.

Indirect costs, also known as *opportunity costs*, can have a signifi-cant impact on your finances, but are not easy to predict or calculate. Opportunity costs relate to the money or investments that you forfeit because of the presence of children. Women are usually more affected by these costs than men are. In order to raise and nurture children, women who temporarily leave their jobs often become ineligible for promotions, lose seniority, and miss out on salary increases.

When I speak to thoughtful couples like Hal and Kristin who would love to have another child but simply can't afford to do so, I wish I had cash grants to distribute! I believe that when you are determining the right size for your family, financial considerations should play a part—but there are many other issues to consider.

Understanding Your Motivations

Back in 1979, researchers Lois Wladis Hoffman and Jean Denby Manis asked 1,569 married women under age forty, along with 456 of their husbands, to answer the question "What would you say are some of the advantages or good things about having chil-dren, compared to not having children at all?" The highest-ranked answers—the essential reasons most people gave for having a child—were love, family, and companionship in concert with "stimulation and fun" (babies and children as a continual source of parental fascination and pleasure). Far down the list were such reasons as carrying on family tradition, achieving a higher place in society, and self-replication.[3]

Today, more than thirty years later, my own research shows that these reasons have stayed pretty much the same: the primary reason to have your first child is that you and your partner want to raise and love a child. And the primary reason to have another child is the powerful love you have for your first child, and the fulfilling, rewarding experience you expect to have as a parent.

Each of us as an individual has an obligation to think about why we want children and what our expectations are. And each set of life partners has the same obligation. Because after thirty-two years as a marriage and family therapist, I've learned that sooner or later, these issues are going to come up—and when they do, they will rock your family, your relationships, and your experience as a parent.

Please take this opportunity to consider your motivations and expectations now. We'll look at three important areas: social pressures (family, friends and colleagues, and the media), your own childhood experiences, and the reality behind your unexplored expectations.

Social Pressures

No matter what your family, your friends, or even the magazines you read say, the choice is always yours: you are under no obligation to have a child, or to have another child, or not to have another child. It is my firm belief that no external pressure should be brought to bear on a couple to have a child or to increase their family size. But that doesn't mean you won't experience such pressure. You will, and you need to be prepared to handle it by understanding your feelings.

Ideally, the motivation to have a child comes from inside, from committed partners whose lives are in sync and whose goals for family life and family well-being are aligned. Often, however, the decision to have children, or more children, is made in response to the needs and wants of others.

Providing Grandchildren

"I never thought about having kids right away," Bryn told me. "My husband and I figured we'd wait a few more years, but my mom and dad kept hammering away: 'When are you going to give us grandchildren like your brother did?' We started feeling really guilty, and finally, I guess we just caved."

"Giving your parents grandchildren" sounds like a nice idea, but the birth of a child to fulfill the needs of the grandparents—who probably have an ideal number of grandchildren in mind!—will not necessarily fulfill your own needs or best serve your family.

Everyone's Doing It

"It seemed like all my friends were pregnant. After Jim and I got married, they kept asking me if we were trying, how many kids we wanted, why I wasn't pregnant yet . . . After a while, I started to panic. Why *weren't* we trying? Is there something wrong with our marriage?"

Starting a family because your friends have children and you don't reminds me of a question popular with mothers everywhere: "If Johnny jumps off a bridge, does that mean you have to?" You don't have to go along with the crowd, especially when it will affect the life of a new person in the world. If you're feeling this kind of pressure, take some time to get to know your own mind before plunging ahead.

Feeling It Would Be Selfish Not to Have a Child Right Now

"Everyone—our family, our friends, the people at work—made us feel like we were crazy for not rushing to have children after we got married," says Andre, who has no children yet. "We said we liked traveling, we liked feeling free, but they're making us feel like bad people who only care about ourselves."

Jen, forty-nine, teaches biochemistry in a Boston medical school. She was hit hard by postpartum depression after her daughter was born, and made the decision to stop at one child despite her friends' comments. "It was hard when our friends and acquaintances asked, 'When are you going to have another one?' There were times when I would find myself almost wanting to mislead people into thinking that we were having fertility problems just so they would leave us the heck alone."

To Give Your Child a Sibling

To many, it seems logical to want to give their firstborn a playmate and companion he or she can count on throughout life. But the goal here is to meet the needs of your actual child, not your own needs.

The perspective that only children are lonely and spoiled has been disproven by numerous research studies. It simply is not true. Bottom line: parents should never feel obligated to have a child just to create a companion. If both parents are in good health, their marriage is sturdy, and they treasure their first child and dearly want another, then having another child is appropriate.

Jen's husband, Marty, says, "We discussed how it would be good for our daughter to have a sibling. Socially and emotionally, siblings are important." In the end, however, they decided that the best thing for the family overall would be to stop at one. (We'll discuss only children more deeply in Chapter Four.)

Feeling as Though It's Your "Duty" to Have Children

As objective and logical as we may try to be about choosing family size, our cultural heritage and spiritual beliefs often come into play. Some religious and cultural traditions favor large families; others frown on birth control. (We'll take a closer look at large families in Chapter Four, and at cultural and religious traditions in Chapter Five.) If your heritage is a vital part of your approach to family life, this is an area to take seriously.

Your Childhood Experiences

Our childhood experiences have an enormous impact on all aspects of our lives. And when it comes to family and children, the urge to replicate the great times we had or to avoid reproducing our terrible childhoods can have a powerful shaping effect on our relationships and families as adults.

Your Own Parents Were Great Role Models

"I have such great childhood memories," Rebekah told me. "Camping and fishing vacations, playing card games as a family, when my dad taught me to ride a bike . . . I feel really fortunate to have parents who respected me when I was little, and I want to be just as good a parent to my kids."

Like Rebekah, you may have been blessed with a healthy, happy childhood. You couldn't ask for better role models than your parents. If you've absorbed their influences, this bodes well for your own family.

Your Own Parents Were Difficult

"I wasn't literally abused or anything, but sometimes it felt like it," recalls Jeff. "They'd be okay sometimes, but when they drank, they drank too much and were pretty unpredictable." I could see that Jeff was still angry at his parents. "Boundaries? They never heard of them. I basically had to parent myself, making it up as I went along. So the idea of being a parent myself is a little scary. I don't have a lot of skills, and I don't want to repeat their mistakes."

If you, like so many people, feel that your parenting skills are shaky, you may want to look for a parent support group. Most communities have resources for parents running their own groups, or groups run by a professional counselor or clinician. Check online or on bulletin boards at schools, churches, synagogues, or supermarkets. If you'd prefer, there are lots of family therapists who can work with you. Ask your medical doctor, friends, teachers, neighbors, or extended family to recommend one; ask for a preliminary session first to see if it's a good fit.

You're Close to Your Siblings

"My mother has two brothers and two sisters," Hal told me. "I have tons of cousins, and I really like that. I like having a big family and having that bond. When we get old, I'd like to think of the kids coming over and visiting. If we had the money, it's great to take kids on family trips and the like. I always thought to myself, I would like to have a big family, too."

"I am the oldest of a bunch of siblings," says Marty, who is hoping to have three or four children. "I tell people that when you have a sibling, you both have suffered through the same good or bad parenting together, so there's camaraderie. I feel fondly about my siblings, and I make an effort to be in touch with each of them."

You and Your Siblings Don't Get Along

"My sister always told me everything was fine until I came along," says Sara, shaking her head. "Then, to her mind at least, everything she did was wrong in our parents' eyes, and I was the princess. That certainly wasn't my experience, but to this day we have a strained relationship. So I'm a little wary of what can happen between siblings."

Uncomfortable sibling relationships can color your idea of what makes a happy family. Not all brothers and sisters get along, either as children or as adults. But your experience as a child will not necessarily carry over to your own family.

Expectations: Myth Versus Reality

As logical as we may think we're being when we consider the perfect family size, we often have psychological and emotional motivations we haven't acknowledged. As parents, we can unwittingly put great burdens on our children to deliver the emotional satisfaction we yearned for in our own childhood hopes and dreams. So many failed athletes, scholars, actors, and business tycoons unfairly try to manipulate, cajole, and coerce their kids to feed selfish needs that are not really the children's responsibility at all.

REALITY CHECK
Gender Issues

Hal and Kristin told me how they felt during Kristin's pregnancy with their daughter. Their experience is fairly typical of that of many parents who are pinning their hopes on their child's being a particular gender.

"I was supportive during pregnancy," says Hal, "when we thought it was going to be a boy."

"We had a feeling it was a boy," says Kristin. "Everyone said that with boys, you 'glow.' Everyone has a theory, and apparently I was glowing. I wanted a girl so badly that I thought to myself, *I know it will be a boy*."

"When it wasn't a boy, I was devastated," admits Hal. "But that lasted one day. So it's a girl, I thought to myself. Okay, whatever! My daughter is a girly girl, but still loads of fun, and athletic. She's a baseball fan, and we love to sit and watch games together. She is truly a daddy's girl. She's a combination of my wife and myself. I am happier with my daughter than my friends who have sons. Boy, what they're going through!"

Expecting that your child will be a certain gender, and conceiving another child with the express purpose of achieving your ideal gender balance, may sound logical—but it's not a compelling reason to add to your family.

First, until technology advances further, you can't choose the sex of your child. Second, if the new baby is not the gender you hoped for, won't that be a disappointment? Settling for second best is not the way to bring a precious baby into this world.

Hope, instead, for your baby to grow up to be a healthy, happy person in his or her own right! And be prepared to love your child for herself or himself, no matter what.

We may also unconsciously expect to receive positive emotional and psychological benefits from our children beyond these social and material accomplishments. It is not uncommon, for example, for parents to believe that their children will be their "best friends," and to feel slighted when sons and daughters turn out to have personalities very different from theirs, or make "unsuitable" friends of their own. Parents may also expect that older children will naturally want to care for younger children, or that they will be loving companions and caregivers later in life. Such expectations can easily strain the relationship between parent and child and interfere with the child's healthy development.

As you consider the common statements in the following headings, think about what lies behind them. Do they really represent what you feel or what might actually happen? Is this expectation really a good reason to have a child?

You Want a Distraction from Your Adult Problems

"When I was pregnant with my first child," says Joanna, "I remember feeling this great sense of relief that I could finally stop thinking about me and whether I should stay in my job, which I hated, and what I should do with my life. I would have someone else to think about! Now that I have two children, going to work every morning almost seems like a vacation, and I am so busy worrying about the kids and do they have what they need and when do I need to sign them up for camp that I almost never think about myself."

Children will certainly distract you from yourself—perhaps more than you suspected. Two children are twice as distracting as one . . . you get the idea. It's tempting to have children because you need a new direction in life. But being a parent, fundamentally, needs to be about your child—not about his or her function in your life. You, me, all of us need to have adult lives of our own.

Remember, children grow up and leave. If you're dependent on them for distraction or any other form of emotional duty, you're only putting off the inevitable—not to mention placing unhealthy pressure on your children.

You Want to Keep from Being Lonely Later

"My husband was much older than me when we got married, and I realized that he would probably die before I did, and I would be alone for who knows how many years," says Chris. "All of a sudden I had to get pregnant. I just didn't want to end up a lonely old lady with no family to love and no one to love me."

Just as we don't know what lies in store for us later in life, we also can't predict what our children will be like as adults. Your child may love you very much, but his or her career may mean that your adult child will be living far away from you and visiting only infrequently, despite your mutual desire to be close. In the worst case, if your child feels pressure to care for you in your later years, he or she may do so resentfully, or run as far away as possible to escape this burden.

You Want to Give Yourself a Best Friend

It's not up to you to be your child's friend—for that task, there are other children. And it's certainly not up to your child to be *your* friend—in this relationship, it's your responsibility to be the grown-up. In later years, as your child matures into an adult, you may be fortunate enough to forge a true friendship; but your primary relationship will always be as parent and child.

If you still think it's possible to be your child's best friend, here's a reality check from Jen: "When I was more available to our daughter during the day, she said that she was an only child and all the other kids at school have tons of siblings—so I was therefore her best friend as well as her mother. But now my work schedule means that I leave at 5:30 A.M. and return at 7:00 P.M. every day. When she wants to really heap on the guilt, she says, 'Now I can't even have these conversations with you!' Of course, she's telling me these things and telling me that she *can't* tell me these things. I pointed that irony out to her once, and it didn't go over very well."

You Want to Replicate Yourself

"Our two boys are nothing like us," Geoff told me. "I guess I never thought about it consciously, but I just assumed—especially because they were boys—that we would go fishing, play Little League, watch sports, do all that boy stuff together. But my older son is a computer geek, and my younger son wants to be a chef. He spends all his time in the kitchen with my wife."

The only thing you can know for sure is that each of your children will come into this world with his or her own distinctive personality. Your children may, of course, be just like your partner or your Uncle Fred or your mom—but chances are just as good that they will be like no one in your family at all. If one of your children *is* like you and shares your values, that's great. But even so, your children will have opinions and personality quirks that are theirs and theirs alone.

You Want to Fulfill Your Own Unfulfilled Dreams

If you always wanted to write a novel, build a business empire, or travel the world, it is possible that your children will live out these dreams. But why should they shoulder these burdens instead of finding their own dreams? It's still possible for *you* to accomplish some of the things you haven't yet achieved. And it is up to your child to discover a whole new set of his or her own goals worth striving for. One of those may be the one you had in mind, but it may not.

Some parents seek to have a child to fill a personal void of self-esteem. Adults with a poor self-image may have a child as a method of creating their own fan club and to augment feelings of self-worth. What better way to do that than to create another human being who is 100 percent dependent on you for everything, starting at minute one? This is not healthy for the child; it is not useful for the parent either.

Another major arena in which this has become evident these days is sports, where parents, rather than cheering on and encouraging their youngsters to be part of a team effort and be healthier through exercise, show their dark side by exhibiting inappropriate behavior or living out the fantasy of unachieved sports superiority. It is inexcusable for parents to attempt to see their own personal dreams fulfilled at the expense of their children's healthy development.

It Will Be Fun to Have Children!

Having children can be a great deal of fun—take it from a father of four. But being a parent also means getting up in the middle of the night when you're already exhausted, staying up and worrying when your child comes in later than expected, having your private time interrupted to settle a dispute between siblings, offering support when your child is devastated by a poor grade or a cutting remark . . . this kind of "fun" never stops!

And there is also some evidence that parenthood doesn't always make people "happy": "Using data sets from Europe and America, numerous scholars have found evidence that, on aggregate, many parents report statistically significantly lower levels of happiness, life satisfaction, marital satisfaction, and mental well-being compared with non-parents."[4]

Your children can give you a great deal of pleasure, but it's important to be realistic. Nothing is fun all the time! My mother-in-law put it this way: "Little kids don't let you eat; big kids don't let you sleep!"

You're Afraid That You Can't Handle More Than One Child

"I never anticipated the kinds of changes a baby would make in our lives," says Nadia. "We're always exhausted! I can't even take a shower alone. I can't imagine how parents of twins do it, and I can't see how I can manage another child."

A not uncommon reason for choosing to stop at one or two children is the parents' feeling that they have their hands full already and wouldn't be capable of handling even one more child. This fear or conviction may be valid, but don't forget you can get help—from your partner, family, and friends; from teachers, coaches, even the older sibling . . . The concept "it takes a village" is quite true. (We'll look more closely at large and small families in Chapter Four.)

You've Made Your Plan

You may have planned your perfect family size from childhood, with names picked out and everything. But real life rarely matches up to fantasy families. (We'll discuss the "ideal" family size in more detail in Chapter Four.)

Share your expectation—whether it's of two girls and two boys, one perfect child, or a houseful of kids. Talk seriously with your partner and see if your fantasies match up. Then be prepared for nature to hand you some surprises!

Try Not to Worry—Aim for Contentment

As the saying goes, "Don't worry, be happy!" But when it comes to parenthood, that's easier said than done.

Kittens and puppies don't raise themselves, and neither do children. Parents are responsible for the well-being of these new people—teaching them the ropes, keeping them as safe as possible, guarding their health, making sure they get an education, imparting strong values . . . a lifelong responsibility that doesn't magically disappear when the child turns sixteen, eighteen, or twenty-one.

Good parents worry about their children. From the moment they are born, and even during pregnancy, we worry about their physical health and well-being. Early on, we worry and ask ourselves,

"How good a job am I doing as a parent?" And then there's the larger worry that no matter how good a job we do as parents, our children might still come to harm because the world is fraught with troubles: drugs, crime, wars, pollution, nuclear disaster, and terrorism. That's a lot to worry about!

If happiness is an elusive state—particularly, it seems, for parents—what should we strive for? Contentment, I believe, is more easily achieved. An inner satisfaction that transcends life's unhappy moments is a wonderful goal for each adult and child in your family.

Considering why you want to have children—understanding your motivations, exploring your reasonable and unreasonable expectations—will give you a firm foundation on which to build a contented family life. When you accept your role as loving parent to each unique human being who becomes part of your family— expecting to be surprised, and willing to be there for the lows as well as the highs of parenting—contentment will be well within reach.

Self-Test
Why Do You Want to Have Children?

Please consider the following statements carefully. If you'd like to use them as a multiple-choice test to get a snapshot of where you stand on various issues we've raised, follow the rating system below. If you'd like to think more deeply about yourself in relation to certain issues, I encourage you to write down your thoughts in a journal.

I also encourage you to consider these statements in concert with your partner. It's a great way to discover how you differ in your attitudes toward children and family, and to find shared areas of agreement that will help make your choices easier.

There are no objective points to add up as you review your responses: your decisions here are subjective. You and your partner will determine the weight of each statement as it pertains to your needs. Feel free to revisit these statements. You may find that over time, your responses will change.

If your responses bring up hidden issues you have never considered, or reveal problem areas in your marriage that need work, I encourage you to seek help. You can find support from family or parenting support groups (run either by peers or by professionals—teachers, counselors, therapists, clergy, or others in the community) or from licensed therapists. Insist that a major focus of the outside support should be the goal of preparing yourself to have a first child or another child, or simply being able to agree, "Our family is complete."

A wise professor of mine once stated, "There are no problems, only projects." If you decide on support or counseling, start soon. Both of your biological clocks are ticking!

Social Pressures

I want to give my parents a grandchild.

STRONGLY AGREE   AGREE   DON'T KNOW   DISAGREE   STRONGLY DISAGREE

All of my friends have children.

STRONGLY AGREE   AGREE   DON'T KNOW   DISAGREE   STRONGLY DISAGREE

People tell me it would be "selfish" not to have children.

STRONGLY AGREE   AGREE   DON'T KNOW   DISAGREE   STRONGLY DISAGREE

I want to give my child a sibling.

STRONGLY AGREE   AGREE   DON'T KNOW   DISAGREE   STRONGLY DISAGREE

My tradition favors large families—it's our duty to procreate.

STRONGLY AGREE   AGREE   DON'T KNOW   DISAGREE   STRONGLY DISAGREE

Your Childhood Experiences

My parents were great when I was growing up.

STRONGLY AGREE   AGREE   DON'T KNOW   DISAGREE   STRONGLY DISAGREE

My parents were terrible role models.

STRONGLY AGREE   AGREE   DON'T KNOW   DISAGREE   STRONGLY DISAGREE

I'm close to my siblings.

STRONGLY AGREE   AGREE   DON'T KNOW   DISAGREE   STRONGLY DISAGREE

I have poor relationships with my siblings.

STRONGLY AGREE   AGREE   DON'T KNOW   DISAGREE   STRONGLY DISAGREE

Expectations: Myth Versus Reality

A child will be a great distraction from my own issues.

STRONGLY AGREE   AGREE   DON'T KNOW   DISAGREE   STRONGLY DISAGREE

I don't want to be lonely later in life.

STRONGLY AGREE   AGREE   DON'T KNOW   DISAGREE   STRONGLY DISAGREE

My child will be my best friend.

STRONGLY AGREE   AGREE   DON'T KNOW   DISAGREE   STRONGLY DISAGREE

My child will be like me and have my values.

STRONGLY AGREE   AGREE   DON'T KNOW   DISAGREE   STRONGLY DISAGREE

My child will accomplish what I never achieved.

STRONGLY AGREE   AGREE   DON'T KNOW   DISAGREE   STRONGLY DISAGREE

It will be fun to have children!

STRONGLY AGREE   AGREE   DON'T KNOW   DISAGREE   STRONGLY DISAGREE

I don't think I can handle one more child.

STRONGLY AGREE   AGREE   DON'T KNOW   DISAGREE   STRONGLY DISAGREE

When Is the Best Time for You to Have Children?

Making the decision to have a child is momentous.
It is to decide forever to have your heart go walking
around outside your body.

—*Elizabeth Stone*

Children change our lives in unexpected ways. They bring us
joy, but they also take work. We worry about them, change
our life plans for them, spend our money on them, and find our
free time filled up with meeting their needs. Although we may
do these things happily and even gratefully, we have to take all
the ramifications of bringing another human being into the world
into account when we are considering adding another child to our
family.

Accidental pregnancies are always a possibility, and most families find the love and flexibility to accommodate and welcome
the unexpected new member. But most of the time, the timing
of adding a new child to the family is up to you and your partner.

The questions in this chapter address the areas that affect that timing the most: age, career, relationship, physical and emotional health, and the knotty question of what's the best age difference between siblings.

Although nature may put some decisions beyond your control, you and your partner must seriously consider these basic issues:

- Is this the ideal time for your family to grow in size?
- Are you really ready to have a child—or another child—right now?

Your Age Now—and Later

I admit to a bias on the side of parenting earlier in life. For one thing, younger parents are generally healthier and have more energy than older parents, and will probably have at least a couple of decades to continue serving as role models for their adult children. And medical science has shown much better outcomes for mothers and children when the mother is out of her teens and not yet thirty. Babies don't stay tiny for long—they grow and grow and grow, and eighteen years later they may or may not be ready to strike out on their own. The Parenting Stages in Years chart (see the Reality Check box) is a good graphic representation of how the average parenting and nonparenting years look.

Of course, there's always another point of view. As we mature, we become less absorbed in proving ourselves and building a career, and more able to appreciate the wonders of family. "I was not ready to be a parent when I was young," says Kenny, who became a father for the first time at forty-seven. "I was still a child myself, totally self-absorbed. I'd hate for my son to have that guy as a dad!"

As you reflect on these questions, you and your partner should think about your ages now, your ages as your children grow up, and your ages when the children will be launched into their own lives. As always, there are no right answers—only *your* answers.

REALITY CHECK
Parenting Stages in Years

This chart, based on data from the 2005 U.S. Census, assumes that you marry at age twenty-five and both live to age seventy-five; you have three children, all born two years apart. The children are at home for twenty-two years, and the two of you are an empty-nest couple for twenty-four years.

Parenting Stages in Years

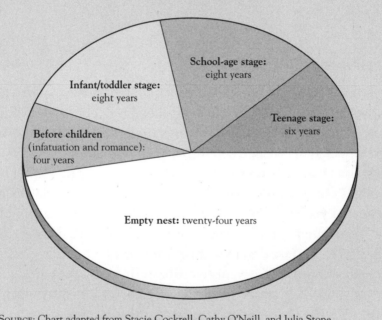

SOURCE: Chart adapted from Stacie Cockrell, Cathy O'Neill, and Julia Stone, *Babyproofing Your Marriage*, New York: HarperCollins, 2007.

Teenage Parenthood

Teenagers, to a large degree, are still children themselves—and I agree that most lack the emotional maturity to be parents. Nonetheless, teenagers do have children. According to the CDC, about one million teens become pregnant each year in the United States, which also has the world's highest teen pregnancy rate.[1]

If you're a teenager who is thinking about starting a family, I urge you to wait—for a number of reasons.

Medically, teens are at higher risk of giving birth to low-birth-weight or premature babies, which can present problems for the child; and although it seems counterintuitive, young mothers are at higher risk for pregnancy-induced conditions like hypertension and pre-eclampsia. Emotionally, teenage mothers run the risk of postpartum depression. And although you will probably grow up fast if you become a young parent, you will miss out on crucial years of maturing that will serve you and your family well in years to come.

Parenthood in Your Twenties

Ozzie and Gail are in their late twenties. They've been married for four years, and have a one-year-old-daughter. They live in Richmond, Virginia, where Ozzie owns an electronics business and Gail works as an occupational therapist. Gail and Ozzie share a pragmatic attitude toward children and family: "The sooner that you have children, the sooner that the children will grow up, and the sooner you're able to have more time for yourself," says Gail.

"There are a ton of things that we still want to do together," adds Ozzie, "and we don't want be doing these things as seventy- or eighty-year-olds. We want to retire as young as we can."

Gail and Ozzie are a thoughtful couple who are pretty much on target with the chart of parenting stages shown earlier. Although, as you will see, they do struggle with adding more children to their family—and life is nothing if not unpredictable—they have a good chance of realizing their dreams.

But even parents in their twenties can feel exhausted by parenthood.

"Sometimes I'm so tired I don't have energy for anything," says Gail. And we only have one baby so far. It takes so much energy just to play with her, and I'm only twenty-seven."

All of us have our own physical and emotional needs. No matter what you may think you believe about when and how many children to add to your family, it's important to respect your sense of your own limits, and your partner's. Ultimately, allowing yourself the time you need to recover will benefit everyone in the family.

Parenthood in Your Thirties

"I was exactly thirty-five when my son was born," says Karen. "He was healthy and perfect, and I felt emotionally ready to be his mom—I shudder to think what kind of parent I would have been in my twenties, when all I thought about was me, me, me!"

If you feel like Karen, you're not alone. Approximately 20 percent of women wait until after thirty-five to begin having children.[2] Readiness, emotional and physical, plays a big part in healthy parenting, and if you don't feel ready earlier, or are not in a relationship that supports having children, waiting is a reasonable and sensible choice. I do, however, caution you not to wait too long in the belief that you always have time . . . your body knows otherwise!

The decision to delay comes with consequences that take their toll on spouses and society. Rates of miscarriage, placenta previa, low birth weight, and genetic disorders like Down syndrome all increase for babies of older mothers. The mother's health, too, can be at risk: older mothers experience higher rates of gestational diabetes, high blood pressure, and ectopic pregnancy.[3]

"I never even thought about having a baby until I was thirty-five," says Ellen, a paralegal from Arizona, "and then I wanted to get pregnant right away. I did—three times. Two of my pregnancies ended in miscarriage, which was a huge shock. It ended up taking me five years to have a child once we started trying, and even though we wanted more than one, it turned out to be impossible. I'd planned out my career really well, but this was something I hadn't factored in."

Parenthood in Your Forties and Older

As long as you're ovulating, you have a chance of getting pregnant. Many late-life babies have been born because the parents were sure they were beyond the need for birth control! And medical advances have now made it possible for women fifty and older to get pregnant.

But should they? For women especially, waiting until they are older to have children is, to a large degree, gambling with nature.

About one-third of couples in which the woman is over thirty-five have fertility problems. Women have a finite number of eggs in their ovaries. The older the woman is, the older her eggs are. Those eggs may be less healthy than they once were, and there are certainly fewer of them. The ovaries, too, may have more difficulty releasing the eggs.

For women, the choice to have children later in life largely depends on the ticking of their biological clock. Some older women do find themselves being mistaken for grandmothers of their own babies, especially in communities where there are very few women having babies over thirty.

If you are considering having a child in your forties, it's important to understand what this may mean in years to come. If you have a child at age forty-five, you will be fifty-five when your child is in the fifth grade, and over sixty-five when she is getting ready to graduate college. This may not deter you, but it is something to think about and come to terms with now.

Says one older mom, "Suddenly you realize you might not be around for your child's wedding, or will probably never know your grandchildren," she says. "So along with savoring and cherishing these long-awaited children, there's a bittersweet tinge."[4]

Janet, now fifty-three and the mother of Cody, an active nine-year-old boy, in Portland, Maine, is philosophical. "Who knows how long anyone has on earth?" she shrugs. "If anything, I suspect Cody is helping us to take care of ourselves and do everything we can to make sure we are around as long as possible—and he has a big extended family of relatives and friends to count on. My husband and I didn't even meet until we were forty, and we feel blessed to have Cody. It's impossible to think of our lives without him."

For men, the choice to parent later in life is less about biology than about stamina. Some late-life fathers report that life couldn't be better.

Jay, fifty-four, and Robin, forty-three, are both financial advisers in Dallas, Texas. They have three boys and one girl, ranging in age from two to seven years old. "I wasn't ready for marriage and children when I was in my twenties or thirties," says Jay. "Parenting is something I just didn't have a clue about. Now people who don't know me assume that I am the grandfather of these children, watching over them in the playground. But I don't care. I'm very involved with my children's classrooms. I probably spend one to two hours each day at my kids' schools before I get to my office. I volunteer and help out so much that people think I don't work for a living."

Jay continues, "When I look back at my decisions to delay marriage and delay having children, I don't have any regrets. If my children decide to get married and settle down earlier in their lives than I did, that would be terrific. And when it comes to my wife, Robin, I kiss the ground that she walks on because she gave me four wonderful children."

"I volunteer myself as a great example of a late-life successful parent," says Ron, a Northern California social worker, who is now seventy. "My kids benefited from my being older—I was forty-three when my daughter was born, and forty-six when my son was born. I had more money and more time, and I had my priorities straighter than I did when I was younger. And I was increasingly more available as a dad. I did everything from child care to new athletic activities that I'd never done before, like ice skating and skiing—all in my fifties to sixties!"

REALITY CHECK
Is Fertility an Issue for You?

Infertility affects 7.3 million people in the United States, representing 12 percent of the women in the reproductive age population.[5] A healthy thirty-year-old woman has a 20 percent chance each month to get pregnant; a healthy forty-year-old woman has a 5 percent chance each month.[6] Secondary infertility—infertility that follows the birth of one or more biological children—is more prevalent than primary infertility. The emotional toll from the long-term inability to conceive a child can be devastating to spouses. Common feelings include frustration, jealousy, anger, isolation, sadness, and guilt. Self-image and self-confidence are affected as well.

Regardless of which spouse has the physical problems, most of the tests and treatments focus on the woman's body. People typically assume that infertility is the woman's "fault," which is not necessarily the case and adds to the stress.[7] Frequent visits to physicians interfere with careers, and the financing of infertility treatments is considerable. In the United States, each in vitro fertilization cycle costs more than $12,000, and many couples require multiple cycles—a financial burden many couples seem to be willing to take on. In 1986, fertility treatment revenues in the United States were about $41 million. By 2002, they had reached almost $3 billion.[8]

Your Job Versus Your Career

When I first spoke to Ozzie and Gail, they hadn't yet started their family. I assumed they would wait until Gail finished her degree before having a child. But Gail surprised Ozzie by saying, "My career is not that important to me."

"He was not expecting that," says Gail. "I chose to pursue a degree in occupational therapy because I can make a decent salary working part-time and I like to help people."

Ozzie, however, wants his wife to have a second income so that all the responsibility for producing an income doesn't fall on his shoulders. "I'm in business," states Ozzie, "and I remember from my dad's business that you have good and bad years. I want Gail's income as backup if I have business problems."

Gail agreed. "If my having a degree makes him feel more secure, that's worth it."

Today, both men and women have options and considerations when it comes to jobs and career paths. The decision of either partner to put a career on hold or end it in order to care for children could have a great impact at some future date if that person decides to reenter his or her chosen field. These issues are far from simple, and the effort you and your partner put into discussing them before the start of a pregnancy will help you avoid sudden, painful decisions later and give you a range of alternatives you may not have considered.

Worries About Finances

As mentioned in Chapter One, the direct costs of children include housing, food, clothes, health care, entertainment, and day care. There are indirect or opportunity costs, too, including the forfeiting of pension, promotion, or seniority at the workplace. And if one parent has to quit her job, cut her hours, or take time off work, you'll need to factor a decrease in family income into your budget.

"Maybe we were being unrealistic, but I think both Kelsey and I were shocked by how much having a baby cut into our financial resources," says Sean, a new father in his early twenties. "You just can't cut back on diapers. And kids keep growing and needing new clothes..."

"We thought that Sean's income would be fine to support us, at least until Oliver started school," Kelsey adds. "But," she says with a smile, "it turns out that babies grow! We needed more room, we had to move, and the only way to do all that was for me to go back to work. We're so grateful that my mom can look after Oliver some days, because day care is expensive!"

Take an objective look with your partner at how your job or career plans affect your family right now. Are you able to set aside the personal time for just the two of you that you need to make your marriage thrive? Are you financially comfortable or struggling? Are you content with your standard of living? Think realistically about whether you have both prepared yourselves for the impact that a child, or another child, will have on each of your jobs.

Concerns with Balancing Work and Parenting

In the eighth month of her first pregnancy, Gail complained about Ozzie's long work hours. "Sometimes he works ridiculous hours late at night, even from home. Then he's exhausted, and we don't spend quality time together. I enjoy time with him. I'm used to it, and I feel like I need it. Now I worry with the baby coming soon, how does everything get balanced? When the baby arrives, it will add another whole level of busyness."

Sensing her frustration, Ozzie responded, "I have made certain work-related changes, and you see that. I have people working for me, and I have a lot of help these days to support me in running my business."

Bonding—the intense connection you feel with your baby—can happen instantly, or it can develop over time. Either way, it's vitally important for you and your children to develop this bond, which will support them emotionally as they grow and will help you become the best parent you can be. So the mantra you hear about allowing time for mother-baby bonding is really true and quite important. The more time a mother and baby have, especially during the first three months (but also the first three years), the better.

The same, of course, goes for dads. Unfortunately, in most U.S. homes "parental leave" is translated as only two or three months—if you're fortunate—of *maternity* leave. It rarely includes the father. When paternity leave is available, it usually doesn't extend for more than two or three weeks. In most U.S. homes, Dad will continue to work full-time and usually not even take the paternity leave that he is entitled to.

The reality is that most dads have to make time away from work to bond with their children. "Often, on the weekends, I think about my workload and want to go to my office," says Jay, "but I wind up hanging with my kids. Any excuse to hang with my kids, I just weigh it and say to myself, on the one hand, I have so much to do at the office, but do you know? I have my kids. And every time I think about going to work on the weekends, I pick my kids over work for sure."

Stay-at-Home Parents

According to the U.S. Census Bureau report "America's Families and Living Arrangements: 2007," 5.6 million U.S. moms and 165,000 dads were stay-at-home parents in 2007. Top findings of the report include the following:[9]

- Stay-at-home moms were younger and had younger children than other mothers.
- Stay-at-home mothers were less educated than other mothers.
- Stay-at-home mothers were more likely to be Hispanic and more likely to be foreign born than other mothers.
- Stay-at-home mothers had lower family incomes and were more likely to be living in poverty than other mothers.

Harriet Nelson making lunch in a housedress, June Cleaver vacuuming in pearls . . . the stay-at-home mom was the staple of sitcoms in the 1950s, 1960s, and early 1970s. These cultural icons were precisely what the early feminists were rebelling against. Heck, no—we're not going to be like them.

But after the newly liberated working mothers of the 1970s, 1980s, and 1990s discovered that after a long day at the office they were still coming home to a full load of housework, dirty dishes, and child care, staying at home full-time and spending quality time with the kids didn't sound like such a bad deal after all.

However, mothers who trade career for home are in for a rude financial awakening. M. P. Dunleavy, discussing Ann Crittenden's book *The Price of Motherhood,* explains that "Most not only forfeit their income, but also retirement savings, pension and other benefits. . . . Economists say that the stay-at-home parent who relinquishes a career may lose about $1 million over the years."[10]

According to the American Academy of Pediatrics, more than half of U.S. mothers with young children work. "In many families today, mothers continue to work because they have careers that they have spent years developing. Some women return to work soon after giving birth because they know that most employers in this country are not sympathetic to working mothers who wish to take time off to be with their young children. If these women stop working, even for several months, they may give up some of the advantages they have earned or risk losing certain career opportunities."[11]

Fathers who choose to be stay-at-home dads while their partners work full-time to support the family are no longer uncommon. In fact, "The number of stay-at-home dads rose to 158,000 in 2009, a bit of a jump from the 140,000 married men who spent at least one year at home in 2008 caring for children under 15 while their wives worked."[12] And a 2010 Pew Research Center study found that "The institution of marriage has undergone significant changes in recent decades as women have outpaced men in education and earnings growth. These unequal gains have been accompanied by gender role reversals in both the spousal characteristics and the economic benefits of marriage."[13]

If you are considering leaving the workplace to be a stay-at-home mom or dad, consider how even the temporary loss of your career or job will affect your feelings about yourself and your worth, and how it will affect your family's well-being—financial and material as well as emotional. How will you feel about leaving the world of adult conversation? How will your family cope without the financial security you bring right now? How will you feel about the inevitable questions you will have to answer about why you chose this path? These are not easy questions to answer, but they are very important to take into consideration.

When Both Parents Are Working, at Home or Away

As more and more people telecommute to jobs, families in which both parents are working at home becoming more common. It certainly sounds good in theory—you're both there for your children, all the time—and for some families, it is good. "I love it that we both have home offices," says Norah, a phone sales rep. "I can be there for breastfeeding, and Jim can pitch in with diapers. We take turns shopping and cooking. And we both get quality bonding time with our baby." Of course, it also means that you are squeezing your work into the hours (or minutes) that your child is asleep or in school.

For dads like Hal, who began working at home as a financial necessity more than a real choice, "being in the same space all day has its pluses and minuses." He and his wife, Kristin, both work at home and take care of their daughter. "It's actually nice when one of us travels for work. For example, I like to *miss* my wife. Being apart is okay because when we come back together, we celebrate. At the same time, though, I wish I could have an office. I'd love to work, do my thing, and then come home.

"I am 50-50 on having another child. Sometimes I say yes, and other times, like last week when my nephew was visiting, I said to myself no way could I handle having two kids and working from home! If you want something to work, you can make it work. But the recession and the depression have really affected our incomes."

Frequently, both parents must work outside the home to support the family. Finding quality, affordable day care—part-time or full-time—then becomes a necessity. Give thought to who will watch your children: a day-care center, a neighbor, a babysitter, grandparents?

Emotionally, you may have mixed feelings about putting your child into someone else's care—guilt about whether you are doing the right thing for your child, and relief at getting some adult time for yourself. If day care is the right choice for you, make sure it will provide healthy socialization, stimulation, and care that is loving, safe, and attentive to your child's needs.

When the Economy Crashes

Ozzie and Gail are thinking about having another child, but Ozzie is very worried about money. "One of the biggest concerns for me now is this financial tsunami that we are currently experiencing," Ozzie told me. "The market collapse has slashed our savings in half. We needed to put down 20 percent on our first house, and that was a strain. We have new expenses related to the house and new expenses related to our baby. There are doctor bills, day care . . . and it all mounts up. I wonder if we can handle another child financially."

Gail is worried too. "Just listening to Ozzie, you can hear all of the additional stress that's going on in his head. I would like to get pregnant fairly soon, but if that's going to make things worse, then how good an idea is it?"

"Wanting your one and only child to have a sibling is okay, but that shouldn't be the only reason for having a child. It can be part of the package of reasons," Ozzie responds. "You have to know where your marriage is and whether you can handle another child."

Certainly, finances are important. In a survey involving responses from eleven thousand readers of *Parenting* magazine, a whopping 71 percent believed that it is important to be financially stable before having a child. But as one reader suggested, "If you wait to become financially stable, you will never have children."

And another reader said, "If financial stability were a require-
ment, only the wealthy few would ever experience parenthood.
As long as two people are ready to be responsible for another life,
and are able to love, nurture, and provide the essentials, their debt
shouldn't matter."[14]

Your Relationship

Everyone agrees that good parenting is vital to raising a family. But
no matter how good a parent you are to your child, a solid relationship with your partner is vitally important to the continued well-
being of your family. In this regard, I have found over the course
of more than three decades of counseling couples that a healthy
relationship between parents benefits children more than good
parenting benefits the relationship.

"I would not have wanted to get pregnant earlier in the marriage," says Gail. "I think it is important that spouses have time
together before the baby comes along, so that they can get close
to each other. We had three years of marriage before the birth of
our first baby. And we enjoyed it by traveling and having fun. It
would have been nice to travel even more, but if we had delayed,
we would have been even older when we had our first child. We
know couples with two children who have gotten divorced. They
got pregnant right away, and it's extremely sad for the children."

Sometimes, the overwhelming love and protection people naturally feel toward their children can shift the relationship balance
in families. "I was shocked by the love I felt for my first child," says
Sara. "I was totally tuned in to her needs. I thought I was being a
wonderful mom, and in many ways I was. But my husband was so
jealous—he felt neglected. I was torn between them. It caught me
completely off guard." When one parent pays so much attention to
the child that the other parent feels abandoned, no one benefits.

When a new baby comes into your lives—whether he or she
is your first or your fourth—your relationship changes forever.
Babies are helpless and unable to care for themselves, and nature

wants you to bond. The child naturally becomes the focus of your attention, affection, and energy. This is good, logical, and understandable . . . up to a point. But if parents forget to refocus attention, affection, and energy on their relationship, they're asking for trouble.

Jackie and Sam have two children, a three-year-old boy and a three-month-old girl. When they came to see me, they were simmering with mutual hostility. "When it was just us and Michael, we were able to get a sitter and have a 'date' at least once a month," Sam told me. "Now we never seem to get any time for ourselves, let alone each other. Jackie doesn't really seem to care."

Jackie was angry. "Sam doesn't seem to know how hard it is to find a sitter for a three-year-old and an infant. I'm breastfeeding, and Lily's fussier than Michael; I can't just leave her with a stranger. I'd feel guilty having fun. I just don't think I could enjoy myself, and it makes me furious that Sam thinks I could!"

Marriage is a voluntary bond, and you have to keep working on it to keep it alive. You cannot assume you will be able to "rekindle the flame of passion" somewhere down the road when the baby grows up. If you decide to have three children, would that mean you will delay rekindling the flame of passion for a decade? Or will you wait two decades, until your youngest grows out of her teenage years?

I am not saying that good parenting is secondary, but that a successful marriage requires more effort. Professor Bill Doherty says it best: "We taught our children that we valued our marriage without devaluing them, that more for us meant more for them, that we were mates before we were parents, and that in the solar system of our family, our marriage was the sun and the children were the planets, rather than the other way around."[15]

Physical and Emotional Health

A woman's general health and health habits affect her ability to conceive and carry a child to term successfully. Her experience with her first child, and her perceptions of other women's pregnancies, can affect how she feels about the idea of having children.

Pregnancy affects each woman differently. Some never feel better than when they are pregnant, but others experience pregnancy as a direct assault on their body. Fortunately, relatively few women actually die in childbirth these days.[16] Still, the discomforts of pregnancy—bloating, weight gain, digestion difficulties, postpartum depression, exhaustion—can make many women think carefully about the pros and cons of getting pregnant again.

In terms of emotional health, it's also crucial for both you and your partner to be as balanced as possible when you add a child to your household—because children leave you less time for yourself, not more. One author says, "If parents are spending more time at work and fathers are spending more time with their children, where does this increased time come from? . . . They are spending less time on themselves. . . . *That's one thing I really need to start working on, just for my own sanity.*"[17]

Pay Attention to Your Physical Health

Your body is resilient, but only to a point. If you let your health slip, either through improper nutrition or lack of sleep, you may become ill. Then you are a less effective parent and partner. Your goal for yourself should always be the best quality of life that is possible under the circumstances. And if you are planning on getting pregnant, your good health is crucial to you and your baby.

If you are in poor health, very underweight or overweight, on medication, or drinking heavily when you get pregnant, your health and your baby's health are in jeopardy. All women who are considering getting pregnant should be checked out by their doctor first. If you don't receive a clean bill of health, you should probably delay the decision to have a child for a while, and involve your doctor in the ultimate choice. Every medication you take can have a direct effect before, during, and after pregnancy.

Pregnancies themselves can take a toll on a woman's health. "I don't look forward to being pregnant again," says Gail. "I don't look forward to having another C-section. I don't look forward to caring for a tiny infant, because it is very difficult. But I do look forward to having another child, whom I will see playing with her sister and growing together as a family."

Postpartum Depression

Jen had been a confident professional woman for a great part of her life. She was surprised by the intensity of unexpected postpartum depression after the birth of her first child, and it left her feeling unable to cope. "My postpartum depression eventually lifted, but it left me feeling vulnerable. Whenever we would have the conversation about having another child, and I tried to imagine balancing everything—work, being a mom to our daughter and a wife to my husband—*plus* another baby, I would sink back into a depression. I put a lot of pressure on myself. I would dissolve into tears at the idea of how to balance everything. Marty knew he couldn't bring up the topic of kids anymore."

Postpartum depression can happen to any woman, regardless of her history of depression. It goes well beyond the short-term "postpartum blues" that new moms naturally feel when they are exhausted, sleep deprived, experiencing bouncing hormone levels, and adjusting to life with a new child. Postpartum depression may affect as many as 20 percent of new mothers, especially during the first four weeks after delivery. They experience agitation, difficulty thinking, guilty or negative feelings about the new baby, and other symptoms of major depression every day and require medical treatment.

Postpartum depression in men is also now being seen as an issue for families. Research published in a recent article in the British medical journal *The Lancet* found that fathers get depressed too, and it can affect the baby in terms of increased risk of emotional developmental problems, such as hyperactivity.[18]

Sleep Issues

We all wish we could get more sleep. But parents, especially parents of babies and young children, have ongoing issues with getting a good night's sleep. The toll of sleep deprivation is not just physical, but emotional—you may feel irritable and forgetful, and find it more difficult than it should be to cope with the strain of balancing the baby's needs with the demands of your other children and daily life.

As the master of your own body, you are the only one who can determine the absolute minimum amount of sleep you need to avoid being a zombie all day. If you feel sleep deprived now and don't seriously address the issue before having a child, you may be lowering your resistance and making yourself more susceptible to sickness when you are introduced to the "parental sleep deprivation" phase of infancy.

A friend forwarded this joke to me in an e-mail: "Why is it that people say they 'slept like a baby' when babies wake up every two hours?" It's true: the eating and sleeping schedule of a newborn often means significantly less food and sleep for both parents. A mother who is breastfeeding must maintain both a balanced diet and sufficient sleep for her healing body and growing baby.

Ozzie, still in his twenties, wonders how older people handle the sheer physicality of parenthood. "I see what it's like now, to get down on the floor with my one-year-old daughter and roll around. Some people are physically fit and can handle this when they are older. Shopping and holding a baby for an hour or two can be really taxing on your strength!"

The inevitable loss of sleep adds to the toll on your energy reserves. If you resonate with Ozzie's feelings on the subject, give thought to the physical and emotional challenges of raising children. Although some parents believe that the children will take care of each other, reducing some of the parents' burden, I more commonly hear that each additional child raises the bar exponentially in terms of additional stress. Consider whether adding another child at this time is truly something you will be able to handle.

REALITY CHECK
Psychological Nesting

A balanced understanding of yourself at your best and your goals for the future is a great launching pad for starting your family or adding to it—before babies and their endearing distractions turn your mind to mush.

- How do you feel about your life right now?
- How would you characterize your relationship with your partner?
- Have your personal goals been met, or are you on the road to meeting them?
- Where do you see yourself and your family five or ten years from now?

If your life feels out of control right now, or your relationship feels precarious, a new child will not miraculously solve your problems. The introduction of a new child will only add more complications and considerably more stress.

Just as "nesting" behaviors like housecleaning and buying diapers involve physical preparation for the approaching baby, "psychological nesting" entails mentally preparing yourself to welcome your new baby into the family and make her feel comfortable and at home. If you were troubled by your responses to these questions, you may want to consider short-term counseling to address your own needs, or couples counseling for you and your partner. Therapy is a safe place to affirm what's working in your life, examine the areas that are troubling you, and learn new ways of looking at life that can help you feel more in control.

Take time now to give yourself and your primary relationship the same sort of love, understanding, and nurturing you plan to give your new baby. You may need nothing more than some quality time for yourself—to think, read, pursue a hobby, watch a movie, listen to music, take a walk, and chill. If you enjoy these activities with your partner, that's wonderful. If you'd rather be alone, that's fine too.

How Far Apart?

The relative ages of your children will play a large role in your family dynamics. Health (theirs *and* yours), sibling relations, and family harmony are all affected. So if you intend to have more than one child, you will soon be asking this fundamental question: How far apart in age should our children be? In my work, when couples are grappling with the issue of how close in age their children ought to be, I generally advise thirty-six months as a wise interval. Let me explain why.

First, let's consider health issues. Pregnancy and breastfeeding take a nutritional toll on the mother's body—and this can have a direct effect on the success of subsequent pregnancies. Research published in the *New England Journal of Medicine* in 1999 determined that "The optimal interpregnancy interval for preventing adverse perinatal outcomes is 18 to 23 months."[19] These "adverse outcomes" include low birth weight, preterm birth, and small size for gestational age. So, in terms of physical health, it's safest to allow eighteen to twenty-three months between children.

The positive attitude of parents toward their children is also affected by how close together they are in age:

- Having two or more children in diapers simultaneously is stressful.
- Having two or more toddlers to keep track of is stressful.
- Having two or more teenagers in the house is stressful!

Anthropologist Dr. Helen Fisher is a proponent of wider birth spacing: "Having fewer children at greater intervals should not only increase their educational potential, but reduce the incidence of child abuse among parents who cannot deal with the problems of rearing more than one youngster at a time."[20] So, in terms of mental health, wider spacing is better.

A crucial issue is the question of how siblings feel about each other. Will children who are close together in age compete and fight all the time, or will they be the best of friends? Will children who are further apart in age have a loving relationship, or will one bully or ignore the other?

According to child psychologist Dr. Richard Woolfson, sibling rivalry is "strongest when the age gap is around two years [and] less intense when the first child is 18 months or younger. . . . [A]fter three years it's also lessened because the older child will have more of a sense of independence and feel more secure in their own life."[21] This means that you can probably achieve a low level of sibling rivalry by having two children in quick succession—but is it the right thing for your body, for the health of your next child, and—to be blunt—for your sanity?

On the other extreme, what's the longest a couple should wait before having another child? Let's consider the dynamics in a family with a space of ten years between children:

- One child enters this world while the other is entering adolescence. (And, as every parent knows, teenagers are in a world of their own!)
- By the time your baby reaches adolescence, her older sibling is likely to be off to college and away from home.

This is almost like having two separate families—one in which the older child has been the center of your attention for ten years, and one in which you may suddenly reframe that child as the perfect built-in babysitter—just when he or she is ready to strike out into preadolescence. You may feel as if you are starting all over again—and you are! The age gap means that the two children will not be playmates, but they may have a close relationship nonetheless.

Still, large intervals between children are not uncommon. They may be the result of a birth control "accident" or a struggle to overcome infertility. As I mentioned earlier, secondary infertility is more prevalent than primary infertility. Researchers are just not certain why couples who conceive their first child without difficulty may have fertility problems conceiving another child.

The same study mentioned earlier, reported in the *New England Journal of Medicine*, also found that women who waited ten years between children were 50 percent more likely to deliver prematurely and had twice the probability of having a small baby.[22] These are the kinds of odds that couples should avoid. So my recommendation to couples, based on this study, is that the *maximum* space between children should be no more than five years.

"I just want to get it over with," Megan told me. "Why be pregnant for years and years?" This attitude is understandable. Many women feel that if they plan on having two or three children, it's easier to have them one after the other. They can reuse their maternity clothes, the crib, and all of the other infant and baby supplies, and they can get back into shape once—not repeatedly. And they can start making plans for the future.

But there are a couple of things wrong with this scenario. In terms of health, we have already seen that having babies one after the other is not a good idea for mother or child. And the idea that you can "let yourself go" between pregnancies is striking another blow against your health, your energy, and very likely your self-esteem.

Another impulse is to replicate the spacing you are familiar with from your family of origin, especially if your sibling relationship is a good one. "I've always thought that a space of two years between children is the best," says Ozzie. "My younger sister is two years younger than me. My older sister is four years older. I had nothing to do with my older sister or her friends when I was growing up, and we were in completely different leagues. But with the two-year difference with my younger sister, I knew her friends, and we were closer and had a lot more to do with each other growing up. I do *not* want spacing of four years between our kids."

You can't go home again. You may replicate the look of your family of origin, but it's a safe bet that your children won't have the same experiences that you and your siblings did. As hard as we try, we can't tweak children's lives to make them exactly what we think they should be.

REALITY CHECK

What's the Optimal Age Difference Between Siblings?

According to recent research by the Meridian Group, "Increasing the interval between births and delaying the age at first motherhood can significantly reduce infant, child and maternal mortality. Optimal birth spacing can save lives and improve the health and well being of mothers and their families. A growing body of documentation supports the concept of waiting three to five years between births."[23]

You and your partner need to make your child spacing decision as a team. If you have time on your side, and if infertility does not seem to be an issue, why hurry this next crucial step in your lives?

Children, as loved and lovable as they may be, inevitably put pressure on a marriage. Why put any more pressure on your relationship than you have to? Let the decision to have each child flow from positive sentiment and a longing to cherish and nourish that child. Take it one child at a time.

Waiting Until "Things" Are "Just Right"

When it comes to adding children to the family, some couples operate on the impulsive principle "Babies are so adorable; let's make one right now!" Others are more cautious, choosing to wait until "things" are "just right." In life, however, we're pretty much guaranteed that there will never be a "right" time for having a child—maybe for millionaires but not for everyday couples struggling to survive.

Money comes and goes, careers change, and the unexpected always happens. Yet, even though there may never be a perfect moment for you to add to your family, with careful consideration of your own circumstances, you and your partner will find your own best time—whether it's your first child or the next of many to come.

REALITY CHECK
The Possibility of Multiples

No matter how carefully you plan for one child, nature may have other ideas. Twins, or multiples like triplets and quadruplets, are always a possibility.

According to the CDC, the birth rate for twins in the United States has risen steadily. "Two related trends have been closely associated with the rise in multiple births over the last two decades: the older age at childbearing (women in their thirties are more likely than younger women to conceive multiples spontaneously) and the widening use of fertility therapies."[24] Research has also found that the parents of multiples are more likely to divorce, largely for financial reasons.[25]

These statistics tell us that attention to your primary relationship—the one between you and your partner—is more important than ever in keeping your family strong and vital.

Self-Test
When Is the Best Time for You to Have Children?

Please consider the following statements carefully. If you'd like to use them as a multiple-choice test to get a snapshot of where you stand on various issues we've raised, follow the rating system below. If you'd like to think more deeply about yourself in relation to certain issues, I encourage you to write down your thoughts in a journal.

I also encourage you to consider these statements in concert with your partner. It's a great way to discover how you differ in your attitudes toward children and family, and to find shared areas of agreement that will help make your choices easier.

There are no objective points to add up as you review your responses: your decisions here are subjective. You and your partner will determine the weight of each statement as it pertains to your needs. Feel free to revisit these statements. You may find that over time, your responses will change.

If your responses bring up hidden issues you have never considered, or reveal problem areas in your marriage that need work, I encourage you to seek help. You can find support from family or parenting support groups (run either by peers or by professionals—teachers, counselors, therapists, clergy, or others in the community) or from licensed therapists. Insist that a major focus of the outside support should be the goal of preparing yourself to have a first child or another child, or simply being able to agree, "Our family is complete."

A wise professor of mine once stated, "There are no problems, only projects." If you decide on support or counseling, start soon. Both of your biological clocks are ticking!

Your Age Now—and Later

I'm too young to have children—I'm not even twenty.

STRONGLY AGREE   AGREE   DON'T KNOW   DISAGREE   STRONGLY DISAGREE

I'm in my twenties, and I'm ready to start a family now.

STRONGLY AGREE   AGREE   DON'T KNOW   DISAGREE   STRONGLY DISAGREE

I'm in my twenties, and I'm tired all the time.

STRONGLY AGREE   AGREE   DON'T KNOW   DISAGREE   STRONGLY DISAGREE

I'm only in my thirties—I've got a few more years before I have to worry about fertility.

STRONGLY AGREE   AGREE   DON'T KNOW   DISAGREE   STRONGLY DISAGREE

I'm over forty—I don't think I can even get pregnant at my age.

STRONGLY AGREE   AGREE   DON'T KNOW   DISAGREE   STRONGLY DISAGREE

I'm too old to have children—I don't want to be mistaken for my child's grandparent!

STRONGLY AGREE   AGREE   DON'T KNOW   DISAGREE   STRONGLY DISAGREE

Your Job Versus Your Career

I'm really busy at work; it's hard to get enough time for my family as it is.

STRONGLY AGREE   AGREE   DON'T KNOW   DISAGREE   STRONGLY DISAGREE

We both plan to take time off work to bond with the new baby.

STRONGLY AGREE   AGREE   DON'T KNOW   DISAGREE   STRONGLY DISAGREE

I'm thinking about giving up my job and being a stay-at-home parent.

STRONGLY AGREE   AGREE   DON'T KNOW   DISAGREE   STRONGLY DISAGREE

We'll both work at home.

STRONGLY AGREE   AGREE   DON'T KNOW   DISAGREE   STRONGLY DISAGREE

We'll both go back to work, and the children will be in day care all day or with a babysitter.

STRONGLY AGREE   AGREE   DON'T KNOW   DISAGREE   STRONGLY DISAGREE

I'm not sure we're earning enough to afford another child.

STRONGLY AGREE   AGREE   DON'T KNOW   DISAGREE   STRONGLY DISAGREE

Your Relationship

We need time together as a couple before we have children.

STRONGLY AGREE   AGREE   DON'T KNOW   DISAGREE   STRONGLY DISAGREE

My children are my first priority—my partner needs to understand that.

STRONGLY AGREE   AGREE   DON'T KNOW   DISAGREE   STRONGLY DISAGREE

Physical and Emotional Health

I've been healthier . . . but I'm sure I'd feel better if I were pregnant.

STRONGLY AGREE   AGREE   DON'T KNOW   DISAGREE   STRONGLY DISAGREE

My last pregnancy was so difficult that I wonder if I can go through that again.

STRONGLY AGREE   AGREE   DON'T KNOW   DISAGREE   STRONGLY DISAGREE

I'm afraid of postpartum depression.

STRONGLY AGREE   AGREE   DON'T KNOW   DISAGREE   STRONGLY DISAGREE

I don't know if I can handle raising another child—I'm already exhausted.

STRONGLY AGREE   AGREE   DON'T KNOW   DISAGREE   STRONGLY DISAGREE

How Far Apart?

I just want to get it over with—why be pregnant for years and years?

STRONGLY AGREE   AGREE   DON'T KNOW   DISAGREE   STRONGLY DISAGREE

My own siblings were perfectly spaced, and I want to replicate that.

STRONGLY AGREE   AGREE   DON'T KNOW   DISAGREE   STRONGLY DISAGREE

We want one more, but I don't know what we'll do if it's twins!

STRONGLY AGREE   AGREE   DON'T KNOW   DISAGREE   STRONGLY DISAGREE

CHAPTER 3

How Many Children Can Your Relationship Hold?

> We fall in love with each other before we fall in
> love with our kids. After they leave home, we will
> still have each other, or so we hope. Our children
> rely on the stability and security of our marriage for
> their own stability and security.
>
> —*Bill Doherty*[1]

One of the most important questions I ask couples in therapy is how many children they plan on having. I ask because I worry that if they have problems with their marriage or children now, the last thing they need is to add more children.

Vicki and Ian are working parents in their midthirties with a two-year-old son and a four-year-old daughter. "First of all," says Vicki, "our children were both colicky. Second of all, they're just difficult children to raise."

Ian nods vigorously in agreement. "For their first four months, both of our children were, well, horrible. We had to hire a night nurse. And our children are very willful. They don't listen well and tend to scream a lot. Taking them out in public is a pain in the neck. Traveling with them is a nightmare. And," he says, with a glance at his wife, "Vicki and I disagree strongly about parenting principles."

Yet despite these admitted difficulties, and despite the fact that both parents work full-time—Vicki is an accountant for an oil company, and Ian is an aerospace engineer—Vicki is well into her third pregnancy. I was curious why parents struggling this much with two children, full-time careers, and a clearly challenged relationship wanted one more child.

"We always planned on three," Vicki says. Originally, she had wanted four children, because she was one of four happy siblings, and Ian wanted three for the same reason.

"But I told Vicki that I wanted two and that I would split the difference, making it three. Of course," Ian said, grinning, "that turned out to be an exact reflection of *my* family of origin." Vicki and Ian were determined to stick to that plan regardless of how much their relationship diverged from their original idyllic vision.

Amy and Wayne, also in their midthirties, have a different approach to family size, one that gives me more hope for the success of their relationship over the long term. They currently have two young children, an infant daughter and a young son who "adores his baby sister." Like Vicki and Ian's son and daughter, however, their children are not perfect.

"The first six months of my daughter's life were challenging," says Amy. "Our daughter was colicky at first, and balancing life and work was a tremendous challenge. We both worked full-time, and Wayne often travels Monday to Thursday. My hours are crazy too. We had a lot of tense moments in those first six months."

When I ask if they're planning on having more children, Amy gives me a wry smile. "From the moment that our daughter was born people said, 'So now you're done. You have your boy and your girl; it's complete.' My husband and I hate that response on a lot of different levels. We didn't—and don't—have an exact family size plan. But lately, we've been talking about a third child. Both of us are in sync on saying that we are not ready to make that decision right now."

I was heartened to hear that this couple was thinking about their family size choices, paying attention to changing realities and considering adjustments that they were or were not willing to make, rather than acting on fixed ideas. Because no matter how many or how few children a family has, its heart is the successful working partnership between the parents.

The Relationship Factor

In my experience, the decision about how many children you and your partner should have ranks right up there with choices about career, religion, and where you want to live. As we've seen, half of first marriages in the United States end in divorce. My many years of personal and professional experience have shown me that family size decisions play a major role in whether or not couples stay married. Well-thought-out family size decisions are essential if partners want a healthy relationship. Such decisions are nurtured by partners who work together.

The arrival of a new baby is usually a moment of euphoria for parents—so much happiness doesn't seem possible. Yet some research has shown that marital happiness *decreases* with the arrival of each child. Whether we accept this or not, the fact is that when a couple has kids, there's less time and energy available for partners to enjoy time together and take care of their own relationship outside of their roles and responsibilities as mother and father.

When I asked Vicki about how her children had affected the state of her marriage, she didn't even have to think about her answer. "I tell each of my friends who are having their first baby that you'll repeatedly think about the word divorce during the first three months of your baby's life—even if you never thought about that word before. Ian is a great father, but those first three months of a baby's life just stunk! At least for me. Ian stayed up with each baby, helped with the feedings . . . and I *still* thought about leaving my family every day for three months!"

No amount of magazines, talk shows, or books—even this one!—can prepare you for the realities of parenting, any more than you can learn to swim without getting in the water. Only when you are fully immersed in family life can you understand the full impact that child rearing has on your relationship. The issues in this chapter are concerned with building partnership and intimacy. As you consider them, make sure your family size decisions are guided by your mission to form a genuine partnership your children can depend on.

Children and Financial Stress

Amy and Wayne are frank about the importance of money and its influence on their decision to have another child. "If one of us is going to cut back on work," explains Amy, "that would be me, not Wayne. He has much more earning potential than I do and no interest in becoming a stay-at-home father. I'm interested in being a stay-at-mom, but I also have a great interest in maintaining our lifestyle. That has been a common topic lately with the economy being as lousy as it is."

REALITY CHECK
How Family Finances Affect Your Primary Relationship

It's a simple formula: the more children you have, the more time, energy, and financial resources you need. Lack of money, and disagreements about how money should be spent, have undermined many otherwise good relationships.

Amy's onto something when she worries about maintaining their lifestyle: as we've seen, it can cost more than $200,000 to feed, clothe, care for, and school a child for twenty or so years. No wonder money so easily becomes an issue between partners! In fact, the Framingham Offspring Study (discussed later in this chapter) found that only one area of marital disagreement is in both men's and women's top three: family finances. And according to a recent survey by the Pew Research Center on what makes a marriage work, adequate income rates fourth in importance—well above children (at eighth place, out of nine areas of disagreement)![2]

Certainly, a comfortable financial cushion can help troubled relationships survive, as Patty and Franklin have learned. Patty, a publisher, has been married to Franklin, an architect, for five years. They have two sons, ages three and one. Patty says that her husband was fine with their first son, but that "he couldn't bond with the baby. I was nursing the baby and he was acting like, 'You're with this baby all the time, and I don't even know this baby. Your being with the baby really means that you have nothing for me.'

"That was very hard for me," Patty continues. "I remember when Franklin traveled for business overseas for a week, and the baby was three weeks old. He arrives home at 10:30 at night and says, 'I really want to go out to dinner.' I couldn't believe he was saying that. The baby was only three weeks old! I told him I was already in bed and I wasn't going out for dinner. His response? 'You never have time for me. You're always nursing; you're always taking care of the children.'

"I got mad at him, but when I gave it more thought, I knew he was really saying to me, 'I need you, and you are not here for me.' The idea just popped into my mind: *we need a full-time nanny.* I knew we could afford it, and I needed the help. And it works! We get more time together, and our marriage has definitely benefited. It's still a lot of work, but it's better now, by far."

Patty and Franklin are fortunate to have enough money to hire a nanny when they need one. Many who don't have the same financial resources, however, are stuck. Parents learn from day one that babies and young children require adults to do everything that kids are too young to do for themselves: make decisions about such basic life needs as eating, sleeping, and getting dressed; comfort them when they are uncomfortable; keep them safe. As Jay Belsky and John Kelly point out, couples must confront such issues "on an almost hourly basis."[3] This is a huge task that means loss of sleep and loss of personal time. It's exhausting, and hiring a nanny to help is beyond the budget of most young couples. Too often, no matter how well intentioned a couple may be, if there's not enough money to go around, one parent eventually becomes a helper rather than a full partner in this process.

Rachel and Eduardo, both twenty-six, are the parents of two young girls, ages one and three. They live in New York City, where Eduardo is working as a sous-chef and Rachel is thinking about going to nursing school. "I wanted to be a librarian," she says with a wry smile, "but libraries are closing right and left, and I heard that nurses can always get a job . . . and it looks like I will always need a job!" They want to move out of their cramped one-room student apartment, but getting the money together has been tough. They fell in love and got married with the intention of having their children right away. But Eduardo says they didn't really think it through. "Rachel was worried that she was at her most fertile now, and having children was really important to her. She didn't want to take any chances. We just figured we'd handle it. We were young and fun, and we'd be great playmates for our kids. But parenthood turns you into a parent—you have to be responsible, all the time. We spend all our money on food and clothes for the girls, and we can't even afford to pay a babysitter. Sometimes our friends will watch the kids so we can catch a movie, but they have their own lives. We can't really count on them."

"I want to go back to school more than anything," says Rachel, "but right now all I do is take care of the kids while Eduardo's at work. We walk to the park and do grocery shopping, and I'm tired.

Sometimes when they finally take a nap I just start crying. I can't figure out how we can pay for my school and child care and still enjoy our lives or even see each other. I don't want to be a full-time mom forever, but I just can't see a way out."

Sharing Household Work

Lynnie and Jeff are in their early thirties. Lynnie does part-time public relations for a nonprofit, and Jeff runs his own landscaping business out of their home in Portland, Oregon. Downturns in the economy have meant that Jeff recently had to lay off his only employee. They have one child, Justin, now nine.

"Jeff and I never considered ourselves old-fashioned, especially in terms of gender roles," says Lynnie. "When we dated in college, we naturally split the bill for meals and movies. And early in our marriage we split the housework. But when I got pregnant, he was working at a job he loved, and I was looking for any excuse to quit mine. Somehow, we just drifted into an agreement where I had primary responsibility for the house and Justin, and Jeff paid the bills and did the taxes.

"It was great at first, especially because I hate paying bills and even thinking about that stuff. But as it turns out, we just don't have enough money. Not nearly.

"Now Justin is having trouble in school, and it's suddenly *my fault* for screwing him up. Jeff feels like I ignore his ideas about what's best for Justin, and maybe I do. I just feel like I know way more about our son than Jeff does. He's out there trying to hustle more income and has no time for us at all. Where was he for the appointments with Justin's teachers? Where was he at 2 A.M. when Justin had night terrors? I'm the mom, but Jeff's the dad. I'm sick of taking all the blame!"

According to research, the traditional working dad, stay-at-home mom roles—especially for those who didn't plan on adopting them—do not promote a couple's happiness. Stephanie Coontz says, "Once a child arrives, lack of paid parental leave often leads the wife to quit her job, and the husband to work more. This produces discontent on both sides. The wife resents her husband's lack of involvement in childcare and housework. The husband resents his wife's ingratitude for the long hours he works to support the family."[4]

Men who think that mundane household chores are the sphere of the woman are asking for trouble, big-time. If they want their relationship to succeed, they need to do their share of the work at home—and that means more than "help with the housework." A man's willingness to share household tasks helps his partner feel supported and understood, short-circuits resentments before they have a chance to arise, and builds a bank of goodwill. Doing things together is, after all, one benchmark of a healthy relationship. And there is a payoff. Psychologist John Gottman's findings point to a connection between laundry and intimacy: "Women find a man's willingness to do housework extremely erotic. When the husband does his share to maintain the home, both he and his wife report a more satisfying sex life than in marriages where the wife believes her husband is not doing his share."[5]

Perceptions of sharing the child-rearing responsibilities can vary from partner to partner. One respondent to a survey by Ellen Galinsky voices this common complaint: "My husband thinks we are sharing if he takes the girls to a birthday party and I pick them up. But who bought the party dresses? And who picked out the presents? And who makes the play dates so they would be invited to the party in the first place?"[6]

Partners need to do an equitable share of the work at home—and both partners need to be in agreement about what "equitable" means! According to Gottman, "Inequities in housework and child care have profound consequences for the marital satisfaction of women, which has to affect the quality of the marriage for the men as well. . . . [M]en who do more housework and child care have better sex lives and happier marriages than others."[7]

THE FRAMINGHAM OFFSPRING STUDY: MARITAL DISAGREEMENTS

According to the Framingham Offspring Study, the following are the top reasons that men and women give for why they argue.[8] (Note the differences in men's and women's perceptions of the relative importance of family finances, child rearing, sexual relations, and household chores.)

Men

	Percent	Rank
Sexual relations	9.1	1
Family finances	6.2	2
How to spend leisure time	6.2	3
Child rearing	5.6	4
Drinking	4.4	5
Household chores	4.2	6

Women

	Percent	Rank
Child rearing	9.7	1
Household chores	8.7	2
Family finances	8.5	3
How to spend leisure time	8.1	4
Drinking	7.2	5
Sexual relations	7.1	6

Be Partners, Not Adversaries

"Babies are terrific for when you sit there and think to yourself, wow—she's ours!" says Ozzie. "But most of the time, it is extremely stressful. She needs a diaper. Then a change of clothes, then she needs to be fed. The division of labor creates more issues than it makes things rosy between spouses."

In their study, Carolyn and Philip Cowan found that "the transition to parenthood seems to act as an amplifier . . . turning up the volume on [parents'] existing difficulties in managing their lives and family relationships."[9] They also note that "the seeds of new parents' individual and marital problems are sown long before their first baby arrives. The couples who report having the most marital difficulty after having a baby tend to be the ones who were experiencing the most strain in their relationships before they became parents."[10]

Stephanie Coontz elaborates on the Cowans' research, noting their finding that "the average drop in marital satisfaction was almost entirely accounted for by the couples who slid into being parents, disagreed over it, or were ambivalent about it. Couples who planned or equally welcomed the conception were likely to maintain or even increase their marital satisfaction after the child was born."[11]

When parents are adversaries rather than full partners, the relationship is an unstable mix just waiting to blow—and a new baby can easily ignite an explosion. In my experience, adding children to such a relationship does not have the effect of creating balance— it simply introduces more complications. Caring for your children inevitably means that there is less time for you to relax and talk as a couple, less time to invest in yourselves as a couple, less time for recreation and entertainment as a couple, and certainly less time (and privacy) for intimacy. The challenge is to increase mutual satisfaction as a couple and raise happy, healthy children too. I believe that couples who can work toward the following six goals outlined by Belsky and Kelly have a great chance of doing just that:

1. **Surrender** individual goals and work together as a team.
2. **Resolve differences** about division of labor and work in a mutually satisfactory manner.

3. **Handle stress** in a way that does not overstress spouse, partner, or marriage.

4. **Maintain** a pool of common interests despite diverging priorities.

5. **Realize** that however good a marriage becomes post-baby, it will not be good in the same way it was pre-baby.

6. **Maintain the ability** to communicate in a way that continues to nurture the marriage.[12]

Find a Way to Resolve Arguments About Child Rearing

As we can see in the Framingham Study, women rate arguments about child rearing at the top of the list, whereas men rate it in the middle—below how to spend leisure time. This difference in emphasis and perception can itself lead to misunderstandings. Sophie and Leo, both in their forties, have been married for fifteen years. And for fifteen years they've been having the same basic disagreement. "Sophie's *way* more tuned in to our kids' needs than mine," Leo complains. "It makes me feel like I don't even exist for her."

Sophie's quick response makes it clear that this is not news to her. "I can't believe you're bringing this up *again*. How can I be in two places at once? If they need help with their homework for tomorrow and you want me to leave them in order to play with you in your office softball tournament, what am I supposed to do? I want to play, but really, their homework needs to get done!"

Leo shakes his head. "How can we have a third kid if we can't work this stuff out with the ones we have?"

Eventually, they found a compromise that surprised them both and actually delighted their children: they wound up bringing the kids to the softball game so that they could do their homework with a friend in the bleachers, and Sophie and Leo agreed to help review the homework later, at home after their game, just to make sure it was right.

Do Children Really Make a Marriage Stronger?

In the strictest interpretation, a new baby *might* save your marriage—for a while. According to one study, "The presence of a child or children deters many unhappily married persons from divorcing, at least for a time. The fact that children tend to increase the emotional and financial costs of divorce to both spouses, must still make children the 'glue' which holds many marriages together."[13]

According to another study, "The presence of children is associated with differences in marital structure . . . that are . . . associated with lower marital happiness. The presence of pre-schoolers and especially the birth of a first child serve to reduce the likelihood that unhappily married people will divorce within a three-year period."[14]

So although children may create problems that can lead to divorce, their presence can also either *postpone* a divorce or, in some cases, head it off entirely. As the conflicted marriage continues, children grow to an age where they require less attention. At this point, the contentious parents can have more time for themselves, improve their relationship, and—we hope—revive their happiness together for the long term and avoid divorce entirely. It happens! Nonetheless, it is never a good idea to get pregnant for the sole reason of preventing a divorce. This is not fair to you, your partner, or your child.

REALITY CHECK
A Bias for Boys?

"My husband, Franklin, and I fight all the time, but there's one subject I can avoid. He informed me before I got pregnant the first time that all men want a son," says Patty. "Having a son means carrying on the family name, and it's really important to him. Luckily, we've now had two boys."

Despite Patty and Franklin's problems as a couple, their two sons just may lead them to stay together. Americans, it seems, have a "boy bias." "When Gallup . . . asked Americans whether they would prefer a boy or a girl if they could have only one child, 38 percent say they would prefer a boy, 28 percent say a girl, and 27 percent say it would make no difference."[15]

Economists Gordon B. Dahl of the University of Rochester and Enrico Moretti of UCLA found that "by a large margin, American men who do have a preference say they would rather have a son than a daughter, and this boy bias subtly shapes such decisions as to whether to marry, divorce and have another child. . . . [C]ouples are more likely to stay married if they have sons, more likely to divorce if they have daughters and more likely to have another child if all their children are girls."[16] These findings are supported by other evidence: "Many families with first-born girls . . . are subject to more strain than families whose first-born are boys. In the first four years of our study, couples were more likely to separate if their first child was a girl."[17]

It saddens me that Franklin's attitude is so widely shared. My wife and I are the parents of four wonderful children, three of whom are girls, and I wouldn't have it any other way!

Learning from Experience

Ozzie and Gail are clear-eyed about what it means to have children and a marriage.

"I can see with our one baby that it is clearly *not all about us* anymore. Ozzie and I have a very good relationship, but things come up in life. We are both considerably more on edge, like when the baby cries and life gets very hectic. The more children you have, the more stressful life is. What happens when two babies are crying at the same time? I don't want to put our marriage in jeopardy by having an endless number of kids, like three or four. I am even concerned about having one more child and the strain that it will bring to our marriage."

Ozzie says, "We have the kind of marriage that if one of us is upset about something, we talk it out completely. And 99 percent of the time, we get it out of the way before we fall asleep, which works for us."

Gail adds, "I'm not worried that Ozzie will decide to push four kids on me, because he is very sensitive to how I feel about things. And how we relate to each other is more important than a specific number of kids."

Sex After Pregnancy

"Seth wanted to have sex right after we came home from the hospital with our daughter. I couldn't even begin to think about it," says Helen, a physical therapist in her early thirties. "The labor was intense and painful—I felt like I'd been ripped apart, inside and out. I already had a baby latched onto my nipples for what felt like twenty-four hours a day. It felt like my nerves were living on top of my skin. The *last* thing I wanted was to be touched and to have to reciprocate. But Seth didn't get it. He felt totally rejected, and I still feel resentful that he was so insensitive—and I'm also still exhausted. I haven't had more than three hours of consecutive sleep for over a year. And now he wants another child!"

Intimate relationships seem to sour first and most dramatically for the woman—labor is called that for a reason! She may be exhausted, physically and emotionally, and she may feel depressed. She may feel unattractive and at the mercy of her hormones. And if there is already a child in the family, her attention is spread that much thinner.

I recommend to dads that they be very sensitive to the mom's physical and emotional feelings after childbirth. Please try to gauge where your wife's limits are, and don't take her lack of interest as personal rejection. Remember, intimacy can be holding, cuddling, and other physical contact without the rigors of penetrating intercourse.

Missing the Cuddly Baby Years

No one actually misses diapers and 3 A.M. feedings . . . but many parents miss the physical, skin-to-skin contact of parent-child bonding and the close cuddling they experience only when babies are totally tiny. This wonderful period can't and doesn't last forever.

Inevitably, children grow older and more independent—just as they're meant to. By the time children are two or three, they're toddling off for an adventure, returning less and less for the home-base hug from Mom and Dad. At this time, if you are also missing the closeness you used to have with your partner, the loss of babyhood becomes particularly sharp.

Choosing to have another child is not a lasting solution. No matter how many babies you have, they grow up!

Deciding to Have Another

If you and your partner are feeling a renewed sense of togetherness as your children begin to feel their independence, you may indeed be ready to add a new member of your family—but then again, that may not be the best idea.

According to researchers, "Aging of children is disruptive until the youngest child reaches adulthood, after which marriages become more stable. Arrival and aging of children is an important dynamic with strong implications for marital stability."[18] In other words, unless you both have established effective relationship skills that keep you on an even keel, another new baby can throw your seemingly sturdy ship off course. Spend some time thinking about what *your* relationship needs.

Having It All

So: Is it possible to have both children *and* a successful—even happy—relationship? The answer is yes—if both mother and father treat their own relationship as central to the family's well-being, and treat each other as friends and equal partners.

Writer Ayelet Waldman has four children with her husband, Pulitzer Prize–winning author Michael Chabon. In her controversial essay "Motherlove," she proudly champions a relationship-centered approach to parenting: "My husband will say that we, he and I, are the core of what he cherishes, that the children are satellites, beloved but tangential. And if my children dislike having been moons rather than the sun? . . . I will tell them that I wish for them a love like I have for their father. I will tell them to settle for nothing less than what they see, when they look at me, looking at him."[19]

Waldman found herself vilified on TV's *The View* and all over the blogosphere. But I think she's right. My research and experience with all kinds of couples show that the relationship between parents is the most crucial element in a child's happiness, regardless of how many children there are in the family.

This book is about choosing the family size that is right for you and your partner—the balance of children and parents that feels "just right." Yet despite the intense focus you are putting on this topic right now, putting the same intense focus on your children can easily destabilize your relationship with your partner. And despite the great love you feel and will always feel for your children, I am not suggesting you create a child-centered family.

I quoted Bill Doherty at the beginning of this chapter, and I think this message is so important that I'm going to end the same way. "The greatest danger of having a child-centered family," he says, "is that, when the children leave home, so does your marriage. . . . Our children rely on the stability and security of our marriage for their own stability and security. So why do so many of us resign from being spouses when we become parents?"[20]

Be partners! Be lovers! Be friends! Continue to seek quality time together. Having a child doesn't mean the end to togetherness. Yes, there is considerable research showing that marital satisfaction decreases with the arrival of each child. But this shouldn't become a self-fulfilling prophecy. Despite the distractions, the inevitable disagreements, the stresses and responsibilities of parenting, you can have quality time together as a couple—*if you set it as a priority*.

And as loving partners who respect one another's varying perspectives, you will also be able to think clearly and realistically about whether adding another child to your family *right now* is also the right choice for your relationship.

Self-Test
How Many Children Can Your Relationship Hold?

Please consider the following statements carefully. If you'd like to use them as a multiple-choice test to get a snapshot of where you stand on various issues we've raised, follow the rating system below. If you'd like to think more deeply about yourself in relation to certain issues, I encourage you to write down your thoughts in a journal.

I also encourage you to consider these statements in concert with your partner. It's a great way to discover how you differ in your attitudes toward children and family, and to find shared areas of agreement that will help make your choices easier.

There are no objective points to add up as you review your responses: your decisions here are subjective. You and your partner will determine the weight of each statement as it pertains to your needs. Feel free to revisit these statements. You may find that over time, your responses will change.

If your responses bring up hidden issues you have never considered, or reveal problem areas in your marriage that need work, I encourage you to seek help. You can find support from family or parenting support groups (run either by peers or by professionals—teachers, counselors, therapists, clergy, or others in the community) or from licensed therapists. Insist that a major focus of the outside support should be the goal of preparing yourself to have a first child or another child, or simply being able to agree, "Our family is complete."

A wise professor of mine once stated, "There are no problems, only projects." If you decide on support or counseling, start soon. Both of your biological clocks are ticking!

The Relationship Factor

I already work too hard around the house. Another child will add to my load.

STRONGLY AGREE   AGREE   DON'T KNOW   DISAGREE   STRONGLY DISAGREE

I think I share in chores and child rearing, but my partner disagrees.

STRONGLY AGREE   AGREE   DON'T KNOW   DISAGREE   STRONGLY DISAGREE

The idea of a relationship-centered family rather than a child-centered family makes me uncomfortable.

STRONGLY AGREE   AGREE   DON'T KNOW   DISAGREE   STRONGLY DISAGREE

Be Partners, Not Adversaries

We argue about how to raise our children all the time, but we're thinking about having more.

STRONGLY AGREE   AGREE   DON'T KNOW   DISAGREE   STRONGLY DISAGREE

A child (or another child) will make our marriage stronger.

STRONGLY AGREE   AGREE   DON'T KNOW   DISAGREE   STRONGLY DISAGREE

Having a child (or another child) will make us happier.

STRONGLY AGREE   AGREE   DON'T KNOW   DISAGREE   STRONGLY DISAGREE

Having a child (or another child) will put a wedge between us.

STRONGLY AGREE   AGREE   DON'T KNOW   DISAGREE   STRONGLY DISAGREE

Learning from Experience

I'm still recovering my body and energy from my last pregnancy—I can't be romantic and take care of another child too.

STRONGLY AGREE   AGREE   DON'T KNOW   DISAGREE   STRONGLY DISAGREE

Our children are so big now—I miss having babies.

STRONGLY AGREE   AGREE   DON'T KNOW   DISAGREE   STRONGLY DISAGREE

Our relationship is so solid now that the children are older. We can handle another child.

STRONGLY AGREE   AGREE   DON'T KNOW   DISAGREE   STRONGLY DISAGREE

Small, Moderate, Large . . .
What's Your Ideal Family Size?

> In China, where the law limits most families to
> one, a poll shows that 70 percent of women want
> two or more. . . . The "right" number seems to lie
> somewhere between China and Nadya Suleman
> [who has fourteen children]. And each of us
> believes we know it when we reach it (and we
> know that it's been crossed by someone else).
>
> —*Lisa Belkin*[1]

Stanley, seventy-nine, is a retired history teacher, and Shirley, seventy-five, is a nutritionist. They have eleven grown children—eight sons and three daughters. When I first asked Stanley and Shirley how many children they have, I was puzzled at their vague responses.

"More than ten," said Stanley.

"Not enough," said Shirley.

When I asked why they were reluctant to give me the exact count, Stanley said, "It hurts childless couples to describe the size of a big family, so I don't want to." And Shirley said, "When you quantify the size of a group of children, you don't differentiate individuals, and you should, because each one is a separate person."

Real or Ideal Choices About Family Size?

For many decades, pollsters have routinely asked, "What is the ideal number of children for a family to have?" Some, like Adrienne, a therapist and mother of two, take umbrage at the very question: "The diversity of ethnic backgrounds alone in this nation should provide a clear indication that there can be no such thing as an ideal family size."

Nonetheless (as the "Surveys . . ." box shows), pollsters keep asking and Americans keep answering. Since the 1970s, Americans have stated confidently that two (or maybe three) children are the ideal number.[2]

Look around and you'll see all shapes and sizes of families: from one child, to two, three, and four, to larger families of five, six, seven, and more. Which is too big? Which is too small? Which is just right? And how can we possibly know for sure? Recently, I did my own relatively small survey of perspectives on family size, and here's what I found:

- The smaller the number of children a respondent currently has, the smaller his or her ideal number of children.
- The smaller the number of children in a respondent's family of origin, the smaller his or her ideal number of children.
- Respondents who were never married consider a large number of children to be "ideal."

It seems that when it comes to the ideal number of children in a family, people want what they have and have what they want!

SURVEYS ON THE IDEAL NUMBER OF CHILDREN (1936–2009)

Q: What do you think is the ideal number of children for a family to have?

	Zero	One	Two	Three	Four	Five or more	Mean[1]
Apr. 2009	3	3	46	26	9	3	2.6
June 2007 Gallup	1	3	52	25	7	2	2.5
Feb. 2004 Gallup/ (CNN) USA Today	1	3	49	26	9	3	2.6
July 2003 Gallup	1	2	52	26	9	2	2.5
May 2001 Gallup	1	2	49	27	9	2	2.6
May 1997 Gallup/ (CNN) USA Today	2	2	46	29	9	2	2.6
Feb. 1996 Gallup	2	3	57	21	7	4	2.4
Apr. 1990 Gallup	3	3	57	18	8	3	2.4
Mar. 1987 Gallup	1	3	56	22	9	3	2.6
Feb. 1985 Gallup	2	4	56	21	8	3	2.5
Jan. 1983 Gallup	3	3	54	21	11	3	2.6
Nov. 1980 Gallup	3	2	55	20	9	3	2.5
Sept. 1978 Gallup	2	2	49	23	13	3	2.6
Feb. 1977 Gallup	2	2	50	22	10	4	2.6
Feb. 1974 Gallup	1	2	46	22	14	5	2.8
Jan. 1973 Gallup	1	1	46	23	14	6	2.8
Dec. 1967 Gallup	0	*	23	30	31	9	3.4
Jan. 1966 Gallup	0	1	18	27	27	7	3.3
Apr. 1965 Gallup	0	1	18	28	29	8	3.4
Feb. 1962 Gallup	0	1	16	24	33	13	3.3
Feb. 1957 Gallup	1	1	18	34	27	10	3.6
1953 Gallup	0	1	28	30	29	12	3.3
1947 Gallup	0	1	26	26	29	12	3.4
1945 Gallup	0	1	22	28	31	18	3.3
1941 Gallup	0	1	31	27	27	14	3.3
1936 Gallup	0	2	32	32	22	10	3.6

[1] Means for 1936–1996 were estimated by Gallup.

Source: Adapted from Pew Research Center, "The New Demography of American Motherhood," revised August 19, 2010, http://pewsocialtrends.org/files/2010/10/754-new-demography-of-motherhood.pdf, p. 28.

Like Goldilocks on her visit to the home of the three bears, you'll know "just right" when you see it.

In this chapter, we'll explore issues concerned with small, moderate, and large families. As I hope you're beginning to understand, making choices about family size is not something you can do using demographics or other people's opinions! A better question is this: "What is the ideal number of children for *our* family?"

And the answer I always give is this: "As many or as few, as long as you think it through."

LIFE WITH YOUR FIRST CHILD—AND BEYOND

First Child	Second Child	Third Child
Play classical music to sooth the baby.	Play classical music to sooth the baby.	Buy an electric guitar, teach yourself chords from Pearl Jam songs, and drown out sounds of siblings bickering.
Sleep when the baby sleeps.	Sleep when the baby sleeps and while the toddler watches a video.	Sleep while nursing, sitting in the minivan at soccer practice as toddler watches videos on the portable DVD player.
Accept all offers of help from family.	Accept all offers of help from family, friends, neighbors, and acquaintances.	Offer your spare change jar to anyone on your block who'll take your children so you can go to the bathroom alone.

Establish regular naptime routine, with child in crib.	Let kids nap in their car seats while you're running errands.	Move kids to couch or bed only when you notice they're collapsed in exhaustion on the floor.
Immediately wash and sterilize every single Binky, blankie, or stuffed animal that hits the floor.	Scrape away obvious dirt and give the item a quick tap-water rinse (or a lick) before presenting to child.	Dirt? What dirt?
To create a cozy space, outfit nursery in whimsical, everything-matches theme like Classic Pooh or Beatrix Potter.	Scour resale shops for anything that looks clean.	Nursery, ha! The crib is going into a corner of your older daughter's room, right under the Justin Timberlake posters.
Potty train by 24 months.	Barely potty train by preschool deadline.	Notice that no one has touched the last three packages of Pull-Ups and realize that she must have potty trained herself.
Wonder how you could love anyone else this much.	Amaze yourself that you're able to love two this much.	Worry that you're capable of loving even more kids this much.

SOURCE: Copyrighted 2010 Bonnier Corp. 72893-nlpf.

One-Child Families

"We decided to stop at one child for a number of reasons," says Margie, fifty, whose daughter, Danielle, is now in college. "But none of those reasons are anyone's business but our own! Of course, that doesn't prevent the comments and questions. We used to get the questions about when the next one was coming. Now, at our age, it's clear that we're done. But just last week we moved Danielle into her college dorm and met her new roommate, and the girl's mother said to us, 'Oh, only one? That's so sad—she must be lonely. You must be so glad she has a roommate now—they'll be like sisters!' Danielle, her dad, and I just rolled our eyes. We're used to it. I guess it will never stop."

Maybe, but maybe not. One-child families are on the rise, and for a variety of reasons.

Busting the Only-Child Myths

Only children are lonely. Only children are spoiled. Only children are selfish. Only children are wacky loners. Only children aren't used to being around other kids, having grown up in an adult-oriented household with two self-absorbed parents. Only children are usually depressed and alienated. These are the persistent myths about only children that cause questions like the ones Margie constantly contends with. Yet researchers have found that only children are really no different than other kids: "By and large, . . . the personalities of only children were indistinguishable from their peers with siblings."[3]

It turns out that the stereotypical image of the "lonely only" was popularized more than one hundred years ago, mostly by one man, Granville Stanley Hall. "What he is most known for today," says a recent *Time* magazine cover story, "is supervising the 1896 study *Of Peculiar and Exceptional Children*, which described a series of only-child oddballs as permanent misfits. Being an only child is a disease in itself, he claimed."[4]

But about twenty-five years ago, professor of educational psychology and sociology Toni Falbo and her colleague Denise Polit busted this myth wide open. They conducted a meta-analysis of 115 studies of only children from 1925 onward—tens of thousands of subjects—which "found that only-children scored significantly better than other groups in achievement, motivation, and personal adjustment. . . . Overall the review indicated that only children were comparable in most respects to their sibling counterparts."[5]

The same reasons skeptics give for assuming that only children are spoiled and selfish also explain why they do so well: parents pour everything they have—love, resources, and expectations—into just one child.

The Rise of the Single-Child Family

As the "lonely only" myth loses its grip, single-child families are growing in popularity. "The percentage of women having only one child," Tina Kelley writes, "has nearly doubled over a generation . . . a trend experts attribute to: a larger number of women working full-time, delayed child-bearing and infertility, divorce, concerns about the environmental effects of large families, and perhaps the desire of hyper-parents to focus intently on a singleton rather than feeling harried with several."[6]

Environment, too, can influence the family size decision, as exemplified by Manhattan, recently dubbed the only-child capital of the United States. As Nancy Hass writes in the *New York Times*, "[T]he single-child family is now the most common family unit in Manhattan. . . . In Manhattan, there is virtually no stigma attached to only children. They are as much a part of the cultural fabric of the city as the unique circumstances that, in a word, breed them: small, expensive apartments, a huge parental proportion of women who delay marriage and child-bearing to pursue careers, inadequate public schools, and sky-high private school tuitions. . . . While the percentage of only children in Manhattan is the highest in the U.S., there has been a subtler boom in one-child families across the country. Only children are the nation's fastest-growing family demographic."[7]

The Happy Only Child Continues the Tradition

Laurie, twenty-nine, is a computer programmer living in San Jose, California. Her husband is a third-grade teacher. She grew up as an only child, and is the mother of an only child.

"I know it's not popular to say this, but I loved being an only child. Being around people all the time really drains me. I'm an introvert—I need quiet time alone to recharge my batteries. Growing up, I had friends to play with, and that was great. But when they went home I could do my own thing—read, do art, play music . . . I didn't miss having brothers and sisters then, and I still don't.

"When my husband and I decided to start a family, the 'problem' of having an only child never came up. He never got along with his older sister, and like me, he's a quiet person. We both feel that we manage really well with one child. When our son, Will, was born, our family just felt complete. When he was three, Will asked me if I had another baby in my tummy, and I told him no, I didn't. He just shrugged and went on playing with his Lego."

A Child from a Large Family Has Just One

Jessica and Joseph run a small construction business in Minneapolis. Jessica grew up with an older brother and a younger sister, and Joseph was in the middle of a family of six. After their daughter, Melissa, now nine, was born, they struggled with the question of having more children, but decided to stop with one.

"It was difficult," says Joseph, "especially for me. My brothers and sisters all have lots of kids, and they really guilted me about it. They said, oh, she'll be so lonely, you're going to spoil her rotten . . . on and on and on, for years."

"Joseph's family is pretty blunt," Jessica agrees. "My brother didn't seem to care one way or the other, but my sister was going on and on about babies, and how could I not want another one. And my parents, of course, wanted as many grandchildren as possible! Sometimes I thought I should give in, just to make everyone happy. But we'd look at Melissa and say, no, we're good—and she's really happy."

"That's right," Joseph agrees. "And we have enough money to buy her clothes and gifts, and take vacations, but believe me, we don't go overboard. And socially, she's cool. She's got great best friends that she's known since kindergarten—and plenty of cousins. My family thinks of us as the oddballs, but they can tell she's a good kid."

Jessica and Joseph had good experiences with their siblings, yet still chose to have one child. But another couple with one child has a different background that led them to the same place.

Zipporah has a twin sister, an older sister, and a younger brother. She's married to Thomas, the youngest child and only boy in a home with two much older sisters. Both had troubling experiences with their siblings that made them both want to stop at one child—their son, Malcolm, eleven.

"My twin and I are so close we know each other's thoughts," says Zipporah. "It's a special relationship, but the downside is that we never really learned to make our own friends, and it was a struggle to express our own personalities. Our older sister was jealous and angry when we were born and 'the twins' got all the attention. Plus, our younger brother was very ill for many years as a child, which put a pall over the whole family. Our mom was so busy tending to his needs that she really didn't have much time for us, which gave our older sister more power—and more anger. To this day—we're all in our forties now!—we have a very tense dynamic."

"My family was no bed of roses either," says Thomas. "My sisters teased me unmercifully my entire life, and we are barely on speaking terms now. I guess Zipporah and I more or less bonded over our miserable childhoods. We just wanted to spare Malcolm any chance of sibling misery."

The Unhappy Only Child and the Sandwich Generation

Edina, thirty-four, is a school superintendent, and Charlie, thirty-eight, is a physicist. They have been married for six years and have a three-year-old son and a two-year-old daughter. They live in Rochester, New York. Edina was not as happy about being an only child.

"When I was growing up," she says, "I spent loads of time with my parents. I was very close with them. They made a commitment to be very present for me. I knew that they wanted other children— not just one child. But my mother had a very dangerous condition when she was pregnant with me, and she was told that it would be too risky for her to ever have a second child. I was always told how much love has been invested in me and that I was always more than enough when it comes to children. I resented it a little and felt great pressure as a result of that."

With families getting started later (Edina had her children in her early thirties) and people living longer, more and more parents are finding themselves in the sandwich generation, responsible for taking care of young children and aging parents. Only children like Edina often find it difficult to manage alone, without the support of siblings who can share the load.

"My parents are divorced, and my mother has become very needy on a lot of different levels—and all that responsibility falls only on me. I feel that I have a heavy burden—all of the care for my mother falls right in my lap. But I'm glad we have the two kids, for our sake, and to have any help they might need down the road, like I wish I could have."

Missing Siblings, or Feeling Content on Their Own?

Edina, along with other only children I have spoken to, laments that she has no peer with whom to compare notes, commiserate, and understand her experience growing up.

"I would say there is value in someone else knowing your story," says Edina. "Now that I have two children, I am comforted by the fact that whatever dysfunction Charlie and I will give over to them, they will always have each other to share the burdens and experiences."

Edina continues, "My closest childhood friend, Cindy, knows me and my life so well, but she's still not my sister, and she does not own this responsibility like I do."

Steven, too, missed having siblings to bond with. "When you ask me about what it was like to grow up as an only child," says Steven, "I'd have to say I guess it could be good, but for me it wasn't so hot. There were two parents and one kid—me. I was always outnumbered. Our family was strictly adult oriented. You do what they want to do, talk about what they're talking about, that's it. I was desolate a lot of the time. I had a lot of cousins, and that helped. They really raised me, more or less.

"But at home," he says, "I had no ally to share with, commiserate with, complain about them to, or have a bond with as kids. My parents' priorities ruled—and they were busy and self-centered. Maybe if they'd been warmer people, I'd have a different attitude.

"So what did I do with my life? I had five kids and four grandkids, so far. I guess I overcompensated a little bit, but I'm happy!"

Dave is an outgoing guy who also grew up as an only child. "I was kind of an anomaly in my large, Irish family," he says. "I would have liked a brother or sister, but my parents were older—they met after the war, and by that time they were in their forties. It just wasn't going to happen. They never got tired of telling me that I was lucky to be born at all! But I always had lots of cousins around, and they were like siblings to me, only without the rivalry. It's funny—I also ended up having just one kid—he's twenty-two, and he's never complained about it either!"

Gail, like Steven, was less happy being on her own. "My friends were jealous of me because I had my own room and my own toys. My reaction was, oh yeah, big deal—I wanted to share it with a sibling. Don't get me wrong; my parents took me many places when I was younger, and many of my friends with multiple siblings took no family trips at all. But I felt that I was missing that sibling.

"Being the sole focus of your parents' attention is a negative thing," she continues. "I had no allies, no one else my age around, just these two neurotic adults. My mother was too focused on every little thing I did. I wished that everything was not focused on me, and that there would be someone else to split that attention with. She'd go, 'What are these crumbs doing on the table?'

I would think to myself, *Leave me alone. I need my space. Stop worrying about your stuff so much.*"

Holly had the opposite experience. "I was one of those really mature little kids anyway—people always said I was 'poised'—so growing up with adults was like heaven for me. And my parents were wonderful. They were fun, they played games—I'm sure on some level they were trying to make up for not giving me a sibling. But they never treated me like a miniature adult, and they never relegated me to the children's table or stuck me in front of the TV when they were tired of me. They treated me like an intelligent human being who could be trusted to make good decisions. I never had to compare myself to anyone, and they made me feel confident in myself. They didn't cater to me, but they took my needs into account when they made decisions. I'm pretty lucky!"

How Do You Feel About Only Children?

Perhaps the "only-child question" is really a parent question. Some children are naturally quieter, some more gregarious. Some only children will wish they had siblings; others will be glad they didn't. Parents like Steven's who leave their only child to raise himself or herself are likely to have a lonely, unhappy child who wants someone on his or her side. Parents who are confident in themselves, strong in their relationship, and respectful of their child, like Holly's parents, are likely to have a child who doesn't miss having siblings at all.

We can't predict the future. If choosing to stop at one child feels right to you and your partner, then it's the right decision!

REALITY CHECK
Does Family Size Affect Children's Intelligence?

Some studies over the years have claimed that family size has a direct effect not only on achievement but on intelligence. Simply put, the theory is that smaller families make more intelligent children and large families produce low-IQ children. But these ideas are being seriously questioned. "Many factors, including genetics, are more influential in a child's intelligence," says a researcher who has evaluated the IQs of about eight thousand children.[8]

Researchers Rodgers, Cleveland, van den Oord, and Rowe found that the assumption that large families produce less intelligent children was flawed: "It appears that although low-IQ parents have been making large families, large families do not make low-IQ children in modern U.S. society. Have parents with lower IQ's in the United States been making larger families? Yes. Do large U.S. families make low-IQ children? No. Are birth order and intelligence related to one another within U.S. families? No."[9]

Social scientists are certainly not of one mind on the family size–IQ question. What does make sense to me is the simple mathematics of parent-to-child ratios in relation to time and resources. There really are just so many hours in the day and a finite number of dollars in your possession. It is a clear and simple truth: the more children you have, the less time and money you have for each one.

Regardless of which studies you find the most plausible, no one can say that your youngest child is likely to have the lowest IQ of your children. The more time you spend with your children and the more emphasis you put on education, the greater the benefit for each child.

Two Children

"In this community there is a perceived norm that everyone has two to four children," says Edina. "There are a number of big families in this part of New York. This is a very affluent suburban area that we live in, and with couples that I meet, many are considering their second child."

Although Edina and Charlie are a couple who very definitely make their own well-thought-out decisions, sometimes couples have two children because that's what everyone around them is doing. Whether or not having two children is really "ideal," the following discussions show that many other reasons contribute to making two children a popular family size.

They'll Have Each Other

"Hari and I have similar stories," Laila told me. "We had childhoods that we perceived to be pretty idyllic. Then our parents both had horrible divorces when we were in college. That really influenced our decision to have more children. My husband and his brother are nineteen months apart, and they are very, very close. He hopes that our children will have that same closeness."

Most parents of two children feel good about the fact that if anything ever happens to them, their children will have each other for support and to continue the feeling of being "family." Parents like Hari and Laila, who learned early on that the unexpected sometimes really does happen, feel that siblings will look out for one another over the long term, not just in childhood.

Pregnancy Is Difficult

"I think we'll probably be stopping at two," says Tam, thirty, whose children are four and six. She explains. "I love babies and children, but for me, pregnancy is quite unenjoyable. For my first pregnancy, I was sick all the time, and my second pregnancy was even worse. In the first pregnancy I could go and throw up and be miserable— no other child was depending on me. But when my son saw me during my second pregnancy, he was traumatized by watching me throw up all the time. He would scream and be upset. He is a very verbal child and would say, 'Mommy is hurt, Mommy is hurt!'"

For some women, whether or not they perceive their first child as being negatively affected by their pain, pregnancy is an uncomfortable, seemingly endless experience that they dread going through again. They may be willing to go through it one more time because they so strongly want to have two children, but they have no trouble saying "Enough!" after the second child is born.

Two Kids Are Manageable

When my discussion with Ozzie and Gail turned to family size, Gail, who is an only child, said that her personality is geared to having things at home be very quiet. When she spends time with Ozzie's sister and her three kids, she can't imagine being able to deal with that. Gail explains, "I want more than one child, but the thought of three or four overwhelms me. My sister-in-law is so stressed that she can't even do her hair, and she has three terrific kids."

Mika, an attorney, is thirty-one. She can't imagine having more than two children either, but for her, the issue is work. "The division of labor at home and employment issues are always mentioned first and foremost as sources of great conflict for couples. The second child brings this out in a big way.

"As my children are getting older," she says, "I have *working mother guilt*. My work is fulfilling, but it fulfills a different part of me than the fulfillment that I feel watching my children grow and being part of that. It depends on the day as to how I feel about the debate in my head: stay-at-home mom versus professional woman. At work they're supportive, but the model is not one where there is an interest in giving employees flextime. Two kids are as many as I can handle."

Pressure from Friends and Family

Hal and Kristin, whom we met in earlier chapters, have struggled with their decision to stop at one child, at least until financial pressures let up. Kristin says, "Our close friends will ask, 'When are you going to give her a little brother?' All of our friends have at least two children; we're in the minority with one child. I'm really worried that our daughter doesn't have a brother or sister. I think it's nice to have a brother and a sister. My dad was recently very ill, and it was so nice to have my brother to commiserate with. He is someone who is always going to be there in life with me."

As we've seen before in this book, family and friends can really turn on the pressure when it comes to their ideas about your family size. If you are inundated with this kind of unsolicited "advice,"

it's very important for you and your partner to have time for yourselves apart from these influencers to think about what it is the two
of you really want and can handle, emotionally and financially.

Two Kids = One for Each Parent

Perhaps the reason why so many families believe that two children
is the ideal number simply has to do with balancing the parents'
perceived responsibilities. Here's how Anne Cassidy describes the
family-size decision-making process in a child-centered (rather
than a marriage-centered) family: "A few years ago, I wrote a
magazine story about why working mothers stop at two children.
At first glance, the reasons were predictable; because they could
not afford or didn't have time for more, because two children were
all they could handle, given their careers and their husband's. But
when pressed to go deeper, many of the women I interviewed said
that they could have no more than two because they had to keep
a one-to-one ratio because each child needs an adult's undivided
attention to flourish."[10]

I've noticed that in families with two children, one parent
tends to gravitate toward one child more than the other, and it's
not predictably one sex or another, but varies from family to family.

Three or Four Children

For people living in a society in which two children is the norm,
three or four can seem like a crowd.

"Nowadays, people seem aghast if a couple wants more than
two children," writes Pamela Paul in a *Washington Post* article about
her plan to have three children. "When Elana Sigall, a 43-year-old
attorney in Brooklyn, was pregnant with her third, people came up
to her constantly, she said, to admonish her: 'You've got a boy and a
girl already. Why don't you just leave it alone?'"[11]

Although some couples find themselves with three or four
children "by accident" or because a planned-for second child turned

out to be twins, many couples do choose to have three or four because that's the number that makes their family feel complete.

Looking for Gender Balance

Corinne, the mother of three girls and a boy, said that she was happy with her first three children, but "my husband was really arguing for a boy." She said they could try one more time, but that was it—if it was another girl, they'd love her and so be it. "He got his wish," she says, laughing. "So everybody's happy.

"I know this isn't unusual. Sometimes," she says, "I see families with three older girls and a little boy toddling behind, or three boys and a tiny little girl, and I think, yep, they said, 'Let's just try one more time, honey . . .' and when they got that boy or that girl, they stopped."

I strongly caution couples against taking this approach, and I always try to dissuade couples who say, "Let's just try *once more*, honey . . ." At this time, there is no reliable over-the-counter gender selection drug, and there is always a 50 percent chance that the fourth child will be the "undesired" gender. That is a significant risk of getting what you think you *don't* want, which puts unwanted pressure on the marital bond (a risk factor for divorce) and on the child who is somehow "wrong."

Three Is Way More Than Two

"Three children is, like, *exponentially* more than two," says Fred. "It just never occurred to us when we decided to have one more baby that it would change our lives so much. When we had two, my wife was working part-time. But now she stays at home with the kids all day—all of the money she earned would just go to child care anyway.

"I don't know how she does it. I have to admit, I'm kind of glad I get to go to work in the morning. When I get home, the amount of noise they generate always takes me by surprise. I'm just glad they weren't all babies at the same time—we don't have enough arms between us to comfort them all!"

"I love my three boys," says Samantha, who had one son before having a set of twins, "but the world is not really set up for a family of five. It's one thing to go out for a meal when they're little, but just try to sit two adults and three teenage boys around a table for four! You learn fast that things are sold in multiples of two, so we almost always have one extra of everything."

Stay-at-Home Parents Can Be a Big Help

In 2006, writer and mother of three Jennifer Eyre White surveyed forty-five other mothers of three. Most (thirty-two) were stay-at-home moms, only three worked full-time, and the rest worked part-time. Most agreed that the amount of work created by three young children, and the expense entailed for child care times three, virtually compelled one parent to be at home while the other worked.[12]

Eyre White's separate interview with Dr. Heidi Murley, a surgeon and mother of four, elaborates this theme. After a few years when both Murley and her husband worked full-time and paid for child care, he decided to retire and become a full-time stay-at-home dad. Murley says, "As a career-oriented adult, I strongly support parents who both work, out of either financial necessity or personal choice. However, our family faced specific challenges that made maintaining two careers untenable. And late nights at the hospital just feel different when it's my children's father tucking them in than it did when it was a babysitter doing the job. We're fortunate to be able to have made this choice."[13]

Most parents of three and four children freely talk about the difference in terms of the parent-intensive hours they require. If one parent is not able to stay home full-time or at least part-time, if hiring help is not an option, or if family support is unavailable, a family of this size may not be ideal.

REALITY CHECK
Family Size and Environmental Politics

Stanley and Shirley are the parents of eleven grown children. As a large family back in the 1960s—the heyday of the Zero Population Growth movement—they used to get plenty of dirty looks. Shirley recalled overhearing a woman complain to her friend, "What can we do? They are using up all our oxygen!"

Today, the environmental movement has kept population concerns at the forefront, often to the chagrin of parents with more than two children. "People have no qualms about telling parents with more than two kids that we are selfish and irresponsible. That we're taking more than our fair share. That we're using up the world's resources," says Jennifer Nelson of her experience moving to the San Francisco Bay Area with her husband and three children. "The funny thing is that my husband and I both come from families of four. When we decided to have three children, we thought we were downsizing."[14]

Environmentalist Bill McKibben, author of *Maybe One*, encourages readers not to have more than one child. One of McKibben's main points is that Americans exceed the carrying capacity of our land. One American, he says, is responsible for more waste and pollution than numerous inhabitants of underdeveloped, overpopulated nations.[15]

Whether or not you agree with McKibben, the reality is that Americans will continue to have as many or as few children as they like, and for an infinite number of reasons in addition to concern for the earth. So I suggest that, in the words of Crosby, Stills, Nash, and Young, you teach your children well. I adamantly believe in the power of parental influence as it pertains to environmental consciousness. Ben Wattenberg said it best when he acknowledged that more people may cause pollution, but more people can also reduce pollution.[16] What people do is more important than how many there are.

Large Families

Despite poverty and even starvation across the planet, many people, particularly those living in underdeveloped countries, desire very large families. In a 1999 *New York Times* article, the authors explained why. "For better or for worse, the status of women in many societies still rests on their success in childbearing. In Zimbabwe, the larger the number of children a woman has, the higher the status she enjoys. In Nigeria, traditional celebrations are held for a woman on the birth of her tenth child."[17]

In these societies, a large family is the goal—a badge of honor and a form of social security. In the United States, even though popular culture extols large families like the very real von Trapps of *The Sound of Music* and the fictional *Brady Bunch*, we also gawk at reality television families like the Duggars, who are currently up to nineteen children and counting. Writer Kate Zernike points out, "As families have shrunk in recent years, and parents helicopter over broods tinier, yet more precious, a vanload of children has taken on more of a freak show factor. The families know the stereotypes: they're polygamists, religious zealots, reality show hopefuls, or Québécois in it for the per-child government bonus. . . . [L]arge families are presumed to be either really rich, having children as status symbols, or really poor, living off the dole and completely devoid of culture."[18]

In the United States, where three or four children are commonly considered to be a big brood, families with five or more children are conspicuous, all-consuming—and expensive! Parents of large families feel the pinch, but compensate by being frugal, stretching resources, and adopting an economy of scale. Zernike notes, "A light bulb lights a room, whether they are four people or fourteen. Their children learn not to take long showers, to share space, to appreciate hand-me-down toys, clothes, and books."[19]

Catherine, a therapist, makes the point that money isn't everything. "Large families do not have the financial benefits of the small family. However, some of the benefits are experience in working with others, interdependence, democratic family style, appreciating differences—values money can't buy."

Here's the bottom line: when a wife and husband decide that they are prepared from an emotional, physical, and financial perspective, they have every right to have as large a family as they want. A 1998 RAND survey asked fifteen hundred U.S. residents, "Should people feel free to have as many children as they can properly raise?"; 76 percent of the general population said yes.[20]

Never Lonely or Lost in the Crowd?

Back in the 1970s, a reporter with a bias against large families asked Stanley and Shirley's seven-year-old (one of eleven children), "Don't you feel bad you have so little time with Mom and Dad because there are so many kids at home?"

The boy responded, "Oh no, just the opposite. When one parent is busy, there's always someone else to play with."

Kids from large families often have to contend with these sorts of questions from people who view their situation as outside the norm.

Carolyn is a married mother of four children who owns and operates a child-care center. She has a good deal of experience with large families, personally and professionally. "I believe that the larger the family, the more love there is between the members," she says. "Also, with the proper upbringing, children from large families are not as spoiled and become more independent, functioning, educated adults in society." Speaking about parents who feel that it's better to conserve their resources for one or two children at most, she says, "There is too much materialism around and not enough concern with education and love for one another."

Frances, who is married with two children and employed as a salesperson, agrees. She has nine siblings and speaks warmly of her upbringing. "Size of a family really has to do with the two individuals raising their children. In my generation, families were larger, not by choice, but circumstance. However, ten of us were quite happy and fortunate in many ways. We have great love for each other; poor food was healthy food—plenty of vegetables and simple delights. Having only two, as we do, has different rewards and limitations."

It stands to reason that the more children you have, the less parent-child time each one gets. Shirley, the mother of eleven, disagrees. "The amount of time a parent has is not related to the number of children. I don't subscribe to the thinking that if you have six kids, each child gets one-sixth of your love. You can read a story to three children, and you can take three kids on an adventure hike. A child does not feel less loved because his siblings come along on a trip."

You Need a Good Support System

Gabriel, forty-two, a chemist, has been married to Wendy, thirty-eight, for eleven years. He has one son from an earlier marriage, and together he and Wendy have six children, ranging in age from two to ten. They lived in Baltimore, Maryland, for many years before moving to Flagstaff, Arizona.

"It's not a matter of keeping up with the Joneses when it comes to large families," says Gabriel, who grew up around other large families in a religious community. "Having been surrounded by a positive model of large happy families was a motivator. It was not peer pressure; it was social validation that it is possible to raise really good children in beautiful families with kids who love each other. Our neighbors and friends in Baltimore were kind people who are focused on family relationships and not on material items. That had a profound influence on us.

"We had our twins sixteen months after we had our first child," he says. "We made it through that because there were tons of women who volunteered to sit in our home and hold babies. A tremendous number of people helped us get through that period."

Wendy adds, "My perception of my own capabilities in terms of how many children we could handle as a family or how many children I could handle as a mother was definitely influenced by the context of assuming that I would be living within a religious community that behaved as a support system for that choice. The notion of us being 'out there' living on our own without anyone who shared our beliefs and wouldn't be there to help us is terrifying. That would have impacted our decision."

The Working Mom in Large Families

For parents of large families, the idea that one parent will be the stay-at-home parent is pretty much a given. But for couples like Wendy and Gabriel, who have a helpful support system in place, resuming a career has been possible. Over the last three years, Wendy has been working part-time, and happily.

"As much as I love all of my children very much," she says, "and I am very happy with my family size, my expectations prior to having kids did not include having to give up my career to the extent that I did. I really love having some time to be able to work. It was hard for me to give up my career in the first place, so I'm gradually returning to the workplace."

In some families, when children grow old enough, the stay-at-home parent feels that it's okay to go back to work at least part-time, leaving the younger children in the care of the older kids. Although this can solve the parent's problem, it can create issues for the children. In Little Rock, Arkansas, Rachel Carroccio, twenty-eight, grew up in the middle of ten children. She says the older girls in the family, including herself, burned out on caring for younger siblings and the house while her mother, often raising them alone, worked outside the home. "'None of us [girls] really want many kids,' Carroccio said. 'My brothers, on the other hand, all want to have kids. I have one brother about to have his fifth child.'"[21]

Teresa, a preschool teacher and the oldest of five, was thirteen when her youngest sister was born. "It was a really bad time for my mom," she says. "Our dad left her in her ninth month, and she was shattered. She'd been with him forever. When my sister was born, my mom was depressed and couldn't even get out of bed. So I guess I pretty much raised my sister for the first year."

I asked Teresa whether she and her new husband were planning on starting a family soon. "It's funny," she said. "I love kids, I have a roomful of them every day at work, and I love my brothers and sisters and still see them all the time. But honestly, I feel like I've already raised children. My husband and I plan to travel for now, no strings attached. We'll see how it turns out."

Stanley has a different view. "Someone asked if our first-born daughter, who was followed by many sons, resented being the oldest. I suggested to him that we wait and see what my daughter decides for her own family size when she gets married. Well, she has many children of her own, so the proof is in the pudding."

Chaos Versus Organization

Parents and children often describe their home as one of "controlled chaos" or "joyful chaos"—a continuing cycle of noise, mess, housework, and piles of laundry. Scheduling—of everything from meals to bathroom time—becomes mandatory.

When I asked Stanley and Shirley how they survived what had to be at times a three-ring circus, they explained the importance of being well organized. Each of their eleven children had a job to do, and jobs were rotated monthly. And that system left time for recreation. "If they wanted a day trip on Sunday," says Shirley, "I'd point out their unfinished household chores and give them a time deadline. Things happened . . . zoom!"

Family Is Family, No Matter the Size

I think we can safely say that the truly ideal family size does not exist. Small, moderate, or large—one is neither "better" nor "worse" than another. As always, ideal is what feels right to you and your partner.

Certainly, the success of any family, large or small, is not a function of the number of children it holds. Real success belongs squarely in the hands of the parents. Dr. Richard Weinberg, professor of psychology at the University of Minnesota, explained in *Child* magazine, "Indeed, parents—not family size—have the ultimate power to shape their children's lives. If parents are patient and caring and want to invest in their kids, they can have lots of well-adjusted children."[22]

Kathleen, an accountant and the married mother of four children, has given a great deal of thought to her family size choices. She says, "The ideal number of children for a family is as many as they can emotionally, physically, and financially handle." But I love most of all her response when I asked why she was not planning to have more children. Because, she said, "Four children is just fine!"

And that answer got me thinking. When you reach the number of children that you and your partner say is "just fine," then your family size decision is made—whether it's one child or eleven!

Self-Test
Small, Moderate, Large . . . What's Your Ideal Family Size?

Please consider the following statements carefully. If you'd like to use them as a multiple-choice test to get a snapshot of where you stand on various issues we've raised, follow the rating system below. If you'd like to think more deeply about yourself in relation to certain issues, I encourage you to write down your thoughts in a journal.

I also encourage you to consider these statements in concert with your partner. It's a great way to discover how you differ in your attitudes toward children and family, and to find shared areas of agreement that will help make your choices easier.

There are no objective points to add up as you review your responses: your decisions here are subjective. You and your partner will determine the weight of each statement as it pertains to your needs. Feel free to revisit these statements. You may find that over time, your responses will change.

If your responses bring up hidden issues you have never considered, or reveal problem areas in your marriage that need work, I encourage you to seek help. You can find support from family or parenting support groups (run either by peers or by professionals—teachers, counselors, therapists, clergy, or others in the community) or from licensed therapists. Insist that a major focus of the outside support should be the goal of preparing yourself to have a first child or another child, or simply being able to agree, "Our family is complete."

A wise professor of mine once stated, "There are no problems, only projects." If you decide on support or counseling, start soon. Both of your biological clocks are ticking!

One-Child Families

Only children are lonely.

STRONGLY AGREE   AGREE   DON'T KNOW   DISAGREE   STRONGLY DISAGREE

Only children are spoiled.

STRONGLY AGREE   AGREE   DON'T KNOW   DISAGREE   STRONGLY DISAGREE

Depriving my child of siblings would be cruel.

STRONGLY AGREE   AGREE   DON'T KNOW   DISAGREE   STRONGLY DISAGREE

Only children get high-quality attention from parents.

STRONGLY AGREE   AGREE   DON'T KNOW   DISAGREE   STRONGLY DISAGREE

I'm an only child, and I would not want my child to grow up alone.

STRONGLY AGREE   AGREE   DON'T KNOW   DISAGREE   STRONGLY DISAGREE

I'm an only child, and I miss the support of someone who "knows my story."

STRONGLY AGREE   AGREE   DON'T KNOW   DISAGREE   STRONGLY DISAGREE

I was unhappy with my siblings, and I don't want my child to go through that.

STRONGLY AGREE   AGREE   DON'T KNOW   DISAGREE   STRONGLY DISAGREE

I don't want my child to have to take care of me all alone when I get old.

STRONGLY AGREE   AGREE   DON'T KNOW   DISAGREE   STRONGLY DISAGREE

It's not fair to raise a child in a family of adults.

STRONGLY AGREE   AGREE   DON'T KNOW   DISAGREE   STRONGLY DISAGREE

My pregnancy was difficult, and I just don't want to go through that again.

STRONGLY AGREE   AGREE   DON'T KNOW   DISAGREE   STRONGLY DISAGREE

Two Children

Two is the perfect number of children to have.

STRONGLY AGREE   AGREE   DON'T KNOW   DISAGREE   STRONGLY DISAGREE

Two children are perfect—one for each parent.

STRONGLY AGREE   AGREE   DON'T KNOW   DISAGREE   STRONGLY DISAGREE

Everyone I know has two children.

STRONGLY AGREE   AGREE   DON'T KNOW   DISAGREE   STRONGLY DISAGREE

Friends and family are pressuring us to give our child siblings.

STRONGLY AGREE   AGREE   DON'T KNOW   DISAGREE   STRONGLY DISAGREE

Our careers won't allow us to have a larger family.

STRONGLY AGREE   AGREE   DON'T KNOW   DISAGREE   STRONGLY DISAGREE

Three or Four Children

Small families are better.

STRONGLY AGREE   AGREE   DON'T KNOW   DISAGREE   STRONGLY DISAGREE

Large families are better.

STRONGLY AGREE   AGREE   DON'T KNOW   DISAGREE   STRONGLY DISAGREE

I can't handle any more children than we already have.

STRONGLY AGREE   AGREE   DON'T KNOW   DISAGREE   STRONGLY DISAGREE

I don't feel like I'm done having children.

STRONGLY AGREE   AGREE   DON'T KNOW   DISAGREE   STRONGLY DISAGREE

My partner wants a larger family, but I don't.

STRONGLY AGREE   AGREE   DON'T KNOW   DISAGREE   STRONGLY DISAGREE

I've always wanted more children, but my partner is happy with what we have.

STRONGLY AGREE   AGREE   DON'T KNOW   DISAGREE   STRONGLY DISAGREE

It's bad for the environment to keep adding people.

STRONGLY AGREE   AGREE   DON'T KNOW   DISAGREE   STRONGLY DISAGREE

More children would make our home chaotic—I need some quiet time.

STRONGLY AGREE   AGREE   DON'T KNOW   DISAGREE   STRONGLY DISAGREE

More children would make our home happy—I don't mind the noise.

STRONGLY AGREE   AGREE   DON'T KNOW   DISAGREE   STRONGLY DISAGREE

We just want to try one more time to see if we can get a boy (or girl).

STRONGLY AGREE   AGREE   DON'T KNOW   DISAGREE   STRONGLY DISAGREE

We really can't afford to have more children than we already have.

STRONGLY AGREE   AGREE   DON'T KNOW   DISAGREE   STRONGLY DISAGREE

We really want more children, and we can find a way to afford them.

STRONGLY AGREE   AGREE   DON'T KNOW   DISAGREE   STRONGLY DISAGREE

Large Families

Large families are great—they have more love than small families.

STRONGLY AGREE   AGREE   DON'T KNOW   DISAGREE   STRONGLY DISAGREE

Children get lost in a large family.

STRONGLY AGREE   AGREE   DON'T KNOW   DISAGREE   STRONGLY DISAGREE

More children would mean one of us would have to be a stay-at-home parent, and neither of us wants to do that.

STRONGLY AGREE   AGREE   DON'T KNOW   DISAGREE   STRONGLY DISAGREE

How Do Old (and New) Family Traditions Affect Your Family Size?

Call it a clan, call it a network, call it a tribe, call it a family: Whatever you call it, whoever you are, you need one.

—*Jane Howard*

My first marriage took place just before I turned nineteen years old," Annie told me. "I was way too young. My family of origin was very strict. My thinking was to get away from my home—and I figured that if I were married, I might be taken a little more seriously as an adult.

"I always loved kids," she continued. "I knew all along that I wanted to be a stay-at-home mom while my children were young. My first husband traveled a lot for work, but we had good health insurance and his income was stable, so we decided to have children right away. Having two children is not double the work of one; it's a gazillion times more work! So we decided that's it—we're done. But after twelve years our marriage failed, we got divorced, and we don't speak much these days. But a few years after my second husband, Hank, and I were married, we had the twins, so now we're a big blended family."

I would be thrilled if all people could marry someone they love, work together to make a life, be clear-eyed and open about children and family and what works best for them, put their relationship first, and stay together happily forever. But as we know, the U.S. divorce rate is very high.

Consequently, there are a lot of different kinds of families in the United States today. We may be younger or older when we find our families. We marry, divorce, and remarry, and our families may encompass the children of two former marriages as well as the children of our new relationship. Sometimes, our children have special needs we never anticipated, and we love them, adapt, and keep going. Other times, as much as we desire children, fertility issues may lead us to the path of adopting our children. Americans have diverse faiths and beliefs about how life should be lived. We may have traditions and cultures that support large families, and we may thrive in these supportive communities.

Some say that America is a melting pot—that sooner or later, everyone adopts American values. To a great extent, that's true, as witness the 2.5-child ideal common to both men and women in so many walks of life. Yet as we've seen, religious beliefs, education, and income levels can all influence our ideas about what constitutes the perfect family size. Ethnicity, too, has an influence. For example, according to the Pew Research Center report "The New Demography of American Motherhood," "Nearly half of Hispanic women ages 40–44 with children (49%) have three or more [children], compared with 27% of Asian women. . . . In 2008, 59% of babies whose mothers were 35 and older were born to white women, 20% to Hispanic women, 11% to black women and 9% to Asian women. . . . White women made up 53% of mothers of newborns in 2008, down from 65% in 1990. The share of births to Hispanic women has grown dramatically, to one-in-four."[1]

For some groups, social and economic pressures have a harsh influence on the daily life of children and their chances of growing up successfully and safely. According to the Kaiser Foundation, "African American men are disproportionately represented in the criminal justice system. The percentage of young African American men in prison is nearly three times that of Hispanic men and nearly seven times that of white men. . . . While African American men represent 14% of the population of young men in the U.S., they represent over 40% of the prison population. This figure does not include the number of young men on parole."[2]

These troubling statistics can have very real effects on thoughts about family. "Our daughter is three now," says Grace, twenty-eight and working to put herself through college. "My husband and I have struggled very hard with our lives, and we're doing pretty well now. But we both have brothers and cousins who got caught up in drugs and crime. I'm not saying it's easy for girls to grow up in the ghetto, but I know we were both relieved that our child was a girl. We'd love to have a son, but we're scared to death about his future."

Although Native American families, too, are affected by social and economic issues, these first Americans come at the idea of family from still another perspective:

When it comes to defining marriage or family, there is much variety among tribes. Many tribes have a clan system that is actively involved in childrearing and have elders who engage in family life. . . . One study found that sixty-two percent of Native Americans disagreed or strongly disagreed with the statement that having children was one of the main reasons to get married. This could be because of the communal responsibility of childrearing in some traditions. In the Navajo tribe, for example, grandparents and fellow clansmen—referred to as "brothers" and "sisters"—are considered part of the family and carry the responsibility of family members.[3]

In this final chapter, we'll look at families who fall outside what we think of as the norm, yet whose lives will probably seem very normal, familiar, and perhaps very close to home. No matter what your circumstance, if you have a family, you must still make the choice of whether and when to add another child.

Blended Families

TV's *The Brady Bunch* is a well-known, if fictional, example of two single partners with children—three boys and three girls—merging to create a new, famously successful family. But the Brady family never confronted the issue that many blended families grapple with: whether or not to add another child.

Here's the story of one such couple.

Sam, now in his late sixties, says that he married his first wife, Melissa, "when I was in my too-early twenties. I was totally focused on building my career, and didn't spend enough time with my kids. Melissa and I barely knew each other when we got married. And once we had two little boys, we didn't have much time for fun as a couple. Basically, I was pretty immature."

Sam and Melissa were divorced when he was thirty-one. He says that's when he "woke up to being a better father." Melissa wasn't working and had a house only a few blocks away, so he saw one of the boys during the week and both of them weekends for many years. When he was thirty-eight, "I got lucky and married for the second and last time. My wife, Carol, didn't want to be the boys' stepmother; they already had a mother. Then Carol and I had two kids together—a girl, then another boy. At first the older boys were excited about being big brothers, but then there were inevitable issues and conflicts that we had to work out."

With the arrival of the two younger children, Sam was no longer able to focus solely on the older boys. They'd come over and visit, but didn't get as much time alone with him. The older boys began to feel envious that the two younger kids were growing up in an intact family with both biological parents when they weren't. Sam's first wife, Melissa, had a few boyfriends, but never remarried and in fact started her own very successful business as a caterer with a popular restaurant. This took her away from the home more, so the two older boys felt more alone and neglected than ever for a while, as they went through some difficult teenage years.

Other challenges had to do with all the birthdays and holidays. Who would come to these events, and where would they be held?

"It's taken thirty-five years of trial and error to figure it out so far, and things are still evolving. But things have definitely improved a lot as time has passed and old feelings faded away. Now the older boys have children of their own, so Melissa and I have a powerful mutual interest as grandparents. My daughter just got married, and all the brothers were part of the wedding, including the ceremony, where they each read something about the vows. Melissa was in the audience, too.

"Our son, the youngest, has a steady girl too. Luckily, Carol and Melissa get along well and are very gracious, kind, and compromising with each other. So we switch around: Christmas here, Thanksgiving there, back and forth, and now with other events with the families of the two older sons. It's complicated, but it works."

Sam's story is somewhat uncommon—not all blended families have such smooth sailing. Harold, for example, divorced his first wife (two kids) and his second wife (one kid); he really can't stand number one, but still occasionally meets secretly for travel and sex with his second wife, and has problems with his third. She wanted a child and he didn't, so she gave up and now has her own interests, many of which don't include him. None of the wives speak to each other. Clearly, the idea of a "blended" family is nonexistent in Harold's world. Such is life.

Although it is my belief that deliberate, well-thought-out family size decisions can lower the divorce rate in the United States, the truth is that—whether because of divorce or the death of a one partner or some other reason—families break apart and re-form in new ways.

Blended Families Are Increasing

Just over one million couples get divorced every year in the United States, and half of divorces happen in the first eight years of marriage. That timing means that there is likely to be one or possibly two young children in the family. According to the National Center for Health Statistics, the number of children involved in divorcing families is 1.2 million each year.[4]

So here's how these blended families, or stepfamilies, are increasing.[5]

- More than half of Americans today have been, are currently, or will eventually be in a "step" situation.
- About 65 percent of remarriages involve children from the prior marriage.
- The October 2003 Census states that 3.3 million children are described as stepchildren.
- Fifteen percent of all children in the United States, or 10.6 million, live in these households.

Parents who have been divorced or widowed tend to remarry sooner than adults without children. Because of the difficulty of the first two years in remarriage, I generally advise these new couples to proceed slowly with family size decisions. Wait until you get past that two-year mark to adjust to your role as a stepparent, see how your partner does as a stepparent to your children, and then give considerable thought to the vitality and durability of your relationship.

Custody and the Blended Family

Custody issues, new relationships, and geographical moves all add complexity to the already complicated issues confronted by blended families. Keeping the new family intact while also trying to keep contact with the children from the first family can often have parents jumping hurdles. Sam was fortunate that his first wife and their two sons lived just a few blocks away. Wendy and Gabriel, however, were not so lucky.

"When the divorce was final, Gabriel's ex-wife picked up and moved from Baltimore to Flagstaff, Arizona," says Wendy. "My stepdaughter was so anxious to be done with all of the legal mess, she didn't care whether she saw her dad every other day or not. She just wanted the whole court thing to be over. She was only five or six years old at the time, and it was very distressing for her.

"But for us, there was no question. We followed them cross-country and moved to Flagstaff. It was traumatic to uproot geographically—we loved our lives in Baltimore and had tremendous support from friends and neighbors—and I already had one child and was pregnant with my second. But in this move my children were a blessing. Instead of dwelling on disappointment, I was taking care of other people; I was giving. That is a much better thing to focus on than being in a city that you don't want to be in because of your spouse's ex-wife!"

Having a Child Together to Create a New Nuclear Family

Kenny, fifty-four, is a banker, and Florrie, forty-four, is a psychiatric social worker. Kenny has two daughters in their early twenties from his first marriage. Together, Kenny and Florrie have one daughter, Natalie, who is ten years old. They live in Columbus, Ohio.

"Florrie had no children of her own," said Kenny, "so there was no question that we were going to have a child together. I was all for it. But it created a lot of problems with my being able to see my two daughters from my first marriage. They tried to be nice, but I could tell they resented the new baby, who made it tougher for me to spend time with them alone. Recently, they told me that at first they felt like 'travelers,' coming and going from our family. And their mother, my first wife, was miffed about what she thought was my reluctance to pay for her girls' school tuition and other expenses. I thought I was being fair, though, since she was working and could afford to pay half, as we had agreed.

"Then," he continued, "when Natalie was two years old, the question came up about having another child together. Florrie wanted Natalie to have a sibling, and she herself wanted another child. But I was opposed. I thought it would be too stressful from a financial point of view and also from a responsibility point of view. And my advancing age was a big factor too. When Natalie was born, I was already forty-four.

"My hope was that Natalie's relationship with my older daughters would continue to grow into a strong connection," he continued. "I hoped it would be a complete substitute or at least a partial substitute for actually having a sibling at home. Florrie didn't want me to be stressed about this whole idea, so she conceded—reluctantly—to having no more children."

I asked Kenny if they have any lingering regrets about not having another child together. "Sure. I'd love to have another child, especially if it were a son. But Natalie's relationship with her sisters has developed nicely," he said. "They see each other on a regular basis, and we go on vacations together and spend holidays together. They really love her, and she loves them. They are not together all the time, but I think it's as good as it could be."

Annie, whom we met at the beginning of this chapter, is now a forty-two-year-old civil engineer, and Hank, thirty-seven, is a county sheriff. Annie's two sons from her first marriage are twenty-two and nineteen. Hank, who was raised in foster care, has no children from his first marriage. Annie and Hank have been married for eight years, and have twin three-year-old daughters. They live in St. Paul, Minnesota.

"Five to six years into our marriage," says Hank, "was when we started to talk about children."

"I was okay with no more children," explains Annie. "My boys were getting older and more independent. They were developing their own minds outside of family life. I was enjoying having some time to figure out who I was again. Then one friend made some offhand remark like, 'Well, you're done with the wedding, and you've been married for a while, so it's time to have some kids.' That comment—I am not sure why—really struck me and started me thinking.

"I started bringing up having a new baby in a playful way—just to see what Hank's reaction would be. After the joking phase, Hank said, 'We do need to talk about this.' So we decided that we wouldn't try to have kids but wouldn't try *not* to have them either, and that's when I got pregnant. But three months into the pregnancy, I had a miscarriage with complicated aftereffects."

"The miscarriage was very difficult for me on several levels," says Hank. "We were thrilled that she was pregnant, and now we lost that baby. Another level was the post-miscarriage medical treatment, which almost killed Annie. That was horrible to go through. I saw this as a clear sign from God that this is not what we're supposed to be doing. Annie was the opposite. The doctor said that she had to wait a full year before trying to get pregnant again.

"After the year, we had the discussion again. She was a firm yes, and I was a firm no. That stalemate lasted about a year and a half. It wasn't worth the risk of something going wrong, and I didn't want to think about the possibility of ever losing Annie. I did not want to take that risk. We weren't fighting over this at all; there was no anger whatsoever. I then did some self-analysis and wondered if I was being selfish. The boys were growing up fast, and we were very close to being empty-nesters. The doctor said that she was fine and ready to try again. I double-checked with those doctors about ten times!

"When I knew she would be safe, I started to change my own opinion. I said to Annie that we should stop using birth control and leave this back in the Big Guy's hands, to see what happens. It's just interesting how we seesawed back and forth. There were times when I said yes, let's have a baby together, and she said no. And then there were times that were just the opposite. In the end, she became pregnant with our identical twins. No fertility medications were necessary at all!"

Cementing the Family Bond

Susan D. Stewart investigated the effect of childbearing on parental involvement in stepfamilies and intact families, based on the reports of 1,905 stepparents and biological parents from the National Survey of Families and Households. Her findings "suggest that the addition of a half-sibling is not particularly beneficial to step-children and provides further evidence that couples with children from prior relationships should not make the decision to reproduce to 'cement step-family bonds.'"[6]

REALITY CHECK
Brave New Family

"We decided to have one more child for a variety of reasons," says Meg, who with her same-sex wife, Rebecca, has a son, six, and a daughter, two-and-a-half. "We both come from large families and can't imagine not having kids. We had our son with a sperm donor. When he started asking when he would have a sister or brother, we both felt like *let's do it!*" Rebecca adds, "We feel fortunate, but we don't feel 'special,' and we don't want to be in our own special category of parenting. We're parents and children. We're a family, like everyone else."

We know now that an estimated 20 percent of gay couples have children under eighteen. For the first time, the 2010 U.S. Census will include data about this growing demographic:

- "It has been estimated that one to six million children are being reared by committed lesbian or gay couples in this country. Some children were born to a heterosexual couple and later raised by a same-sex couple; others were adopted, or conceived through a surrogate mother through artificial insemination."[7]
- "Of the 270,000 children living with same-sex parents, about 65,000 are adopted. Most, like other Americans, are in two-child families."[8]

- "A number of professional medical organizations—including the American Medical Association, the American Academy of Pediatrics and the American Psychiatric Association—have issued statements claiming that a parent's sexual orientation is irrelevant to his or her ability to raise a child."[9]

These statements were confirmed by the findings reported in "The U.S. Longitudinal Lesbian Family Study: Psychological Adjustment of 17-Year-Old Adolescents," conducted by Nanette Gartrell, MD, and Henny Bos, PhD—"the largest, longest running, prospective, longitudinal study of same-sex-parented families." The study, which concentrated on planned lesbian families, "found that children raised by lesbian mothers—whether the mother was partnered or single—scored very similarly to children raised by heterosexual parents on measures of development and social behavior." These findings were expected, the authors said; however, they were surprised to discover that "children in lesbian homes scored higher than kids in straight families on some psychological measures of self-esteem and confidence, did better academically and were less likely to have behavioral problems, such as rule-breaking and aggression."[10]

Same-sex parents are almost inevitably confronted by the need to very carefully consider and plan for the addition of a child to their family, whether through adoption, a donor birth, or in vitro fertilization. My guidance for these parents is the same as it has been throughout this book: let your decision grow from the strength of your relationship, and have as many or as few—as long as you think it through.

For example, as we saw in one of the earlier stories, Sam's older boys, despite the geographical closeness and efforts of all the adults, felt unsettled and out of the family loop when Sam and Carol had two children of their own. And Natalie's older sisters, despite their love and affection for her, felt like "travelers" who come and go. This is not to suggest, however, that you should *not* add a new child or children to your blended family, only that—as with any family size choice—you should make certain that it is a well-considered, mutual decision that takes everyone's needs into account.

For some new couples, the question of having children together is a foregone conclusion. When Wendy and Gabriel got married, Gabriel had one daughter from his first marriage. When she and her mom moved, the new couple felt that they had to follow. Today, Wendy and Gabriel have been married eleven years and have six children together.

"My daughter was five years old when Wendy and I went on our first date," says Gabriel. "Having her in my life had really changed me as a person. Wendy says she saw me as very much a 'Dad-guy' because I was really into fatherhood. She was right—on that first date, I still had my daughter's child seat in the car. I wanted to meet a woman who shared my values and my goals in terms of parenting.

"I saw how Wendy interacted with my daughter, and that she was a really good potential 'Mom-gal,' and in that area we were very compatible. I was very excited about that parenting component being a key aspect of our marriage. I was very predisposed to making our marriage very family and kids oriented."

Hank and Annie feel that their two families blend well. "I refer to Annie's sons as 'our boys.' If someone asks further, I will clarify. If pushed, I would say they're Annie's from a previous marriage, but we have pretty much done this together."

"The older boys have a desire to get to know their younger siblings," says Annie. "I tried to allow my boys as much access as possible. I made sure that they knew it was very important to me that they be in this family. It was very important to me that they were at the hospital when our twin girls were born. They had a desire to be here and be involved, which is gratifying. They babysit for us in order to give us an opportunity to go out and have some fun. But at the same time, they really enjoy the twins and spend time together with them. Their desire to be close to their half-sibs is very much a reflection of how close we all are as a family."

Having a Child to Fortify the New Relationship

My advice to blended families is the same as I give to all couples who are thinking about having another baby. Exercise caution and proceed very slowly. Don't have a child just to cement your relationship. Don't have a child because family or friends expect you both to have a child together. You are playing with fire— and as graduates of the divorce process, you know the potential consequences.

Learn from your mistakes. If you think that parenting issues played a role in your divorce, then by all means proceed very slowly and methodically. Be sure that you have learned the skills of being a stepparent. Make sure that your spouse has too. Be sure that despite all the rough edges in life, you really love children and want to bring another child into this world, and that you are not having a child to reduce external pressures.

Kyle, thirty-two, is a carpenter, and Eliza, thirty-one, teaches preschool. They've been married for three years, and encountered a major issue when they grappled with adding a child to their blended family.

"I'm the typical all-American blend of Scots-Irish-German," says Kyle, "and my two sons from my first marriage are the typical freckled blonds you see on every sitcom. But Eliza's African American, and she and her son are both very dark. Maybe if we lived in Manhattan or San Francisco, this wouldn't be such a big deal, but we live in Indiana, so we raise eyebrows wherever we go, to say the least. Our kids have really bonded, although it was rocky early on, when some of the kids in school gave them a hard time.

"We wanted another child so much, but—to put it bluntly— we had to think long and hard about the effects that racism would have on all of us. In the end, though, we decided that after three years together, our new family was solid enough to handle whatever came our way, and that we weren't going to let other people's ideas determine the way we wanted to live our lives. And our daughter is the proof of that!"

Culture and Religion

Cultural and religious factors can play an enormous role in what we think of as the perfect family size and how we plan our families.

"We have a cultural and emotional support system that goes beyond us as a couple," says Wendy. "That is definitely a factor in our large family size. My religious motivation was that the first commandment of the Bible says, 'Be fruitful and multiply.' I lived in a culture where not only my friends had large families, but it was a given that everybody supported each other."

Religious beliefs can have an especially big impact on ideas about family size. Several major religions in the United States—including the Church of Latter-day Saints (Mormon), Catholicism, Islam, Orthodox Judaism, and some fundamentalist Protestant denominations—encourage and support members who have large families.

Joanne is a retired bookkeeper, and Jack is a retired farmer. Married for forty-eight years, they have nine children—from ages forty-nine to twenty-seven—and twenty-seven grandchildren. They live in Simi Valley, California. Their Mormon faith encourages large families. "We wanted a big family from the very beginning," says Joanne. "It's our religious belief that we should bring children into this world and give them an opportunity to have a body and go through the same experiences that we go through."

Zelda, thirty-eight, is a speech therapist, and Hersh, forty-one, is a sales director for a Fortune 1000 computer firm. Orthodox Jews, they have been married eighteen years and have five children, ages five to fifteen, with a sixth child on the way. They live in Lakewood, New Jersey. Although Jews in Conservative and Reform denominations tend to have smaller families, Orthodox and Ultra-Orthodox Chassidic Jews are encouraged to have larger families—in part to fulfill the biblical commandment to "be fruitful and multiply," and in part to replenish the six million Jews who were lost in the Holocaust of World War II.

"To be fruitful and multiply is the bedrock of our relationship," Zelda explains. "We knew that we would have children, but we weren't sure how many. It wasn't a discussion of would we or wouldn't we. Of course we would have children, but our environment helped shape our feelings. We saw our siblings with their large family sizes—my sister-in-law has twelve children—and thought to ourselves that their lives were fine."

Paul and Ellen, practicing Catholics in Galveston, Texas, have nine children. "We know a lot of big families here in Galveston," says Paul. "The big families are typically more religious. My angle on it is that a big family makes you more religious, not that your religion asks you to have a big family. If you trust in God, God provides all the grace that you need."

Does religiosity lead to larger families? According to researchers,

- "Conservative Protestants exhibit differentially lower contraceptive use and higher fertility than other affiliations."[11]
- "Mormons stand out as the group with the highest ideal family size and fertility."[12]
- "Fertility studies show that women with no [religious] affiliation have fewer children than any other group in the United States."[13]

The Pew Forum's 2007 U.S. Religious Landscape Survey sampled more than thirty-five thousand U.S. adults—including Christians, Jews, Buddhists, Hindus, Mormons, and American Muslims. They found that in the United States, "Mormons and Muslims are the groups with the largest families; more than one-in-five Mormon adults and 15 percent of Muslim adults in the U.S. have three or more children living at home."[14]

According to a 2007 Gallup poll,

Religion is related to views about the ideal number of children, with those who have no religious affiliation and those who rarely or never attend religious services more likely to favor smaller families. Catholics are little different from the overall population in

REALITY CHECK
Correlation with Attendance at Religious Institutions

As this table shows, regular attendance at religious services correlates with larger family sizes—not just in the United States, but globally.

Predicted Ideal Number of Children by Religion and Religiosity Across Countries

	No Religion	Less Than Weekly Attendance	Weekly Attendance	Difference Weekly vs. Less Than Weekly Attendance	Difference Weekly vs. No Religion
Men					
Australia	2.39	2.59	3.09	0.50	0.70
Austria	2.10	2.20	2.41	0.21	0.31
Canada	2.49	2.54	2.84	0.30	0.35
Western Germany	2.13	2.19	2.48	0.29	0.35
Ireland	2.56	2.88	3.29	0.40	0.73
Italy	2.14	2.24	2.31	0.07	0.17
Netherlands	2.27	2.49	3.06	0.57	0.79
New Zealand	2.42	2.49	3.26	0.77	0.84
Norway	2.52	2.56	3.24	0.68	0.72
Sweden	2.40	2.43	2.51	0.08	0.11
United Kingdom	2.20	2.25	2.56	0.31	0.36
United States	2.23	2.41	2.83	0.42	0.60
Northern Ireland	2.60	2.59	3.06	0.46	0.46
Women					
Australia	2.35	2.55	3.16	0.60	0.81
Austria	2.01	2.13	2.51	0.38	0.50
Canada	2.46	2.41	2.87	0.46	0.41
Western Germany	2.14	2.23	2.54	0.31	0.40
Ireland	2.99	2.68	3.19	0.52	0.20
Italy	2.72	2.16	2.40	0.24	−0.32
Netherlands	2.49	2.76	3.36	0.60	0.87
New Zealand	2.34	2.48	3.03	0.55	0.69
Norway	2.52	2.67	2.99	0.32	0.47
Sweden	2.38	2.44	2.99	0.54	0.61
United Kingdom	2.22	2.27	2.58	0.30	0.36
United States	2.43	2.38	2.62	0.24	0.19
Northern Ireland	2.57	2.71	3.11	0.40	0.54

SOURCE: Adapted from Alicia Adersera, "Religion and Changes in Family-Size Norms in Developed Countries," *Review of Religious Research*, March 2006, 47(3), 271–286.

their views of ideal family size. Similarly, there is little difference between men and women in views of the ideal family size.

Roughly the same percentages of Protestants (56%) and Catholics (54%) say a smaller family is ideal, while about one-third of each group says a larger family is ideal. Those with no religious affiliation are much more likely to say a smaller family is ideal, with 70% preferring two children or fewer and 21% preferring three or more children.[15]

The following figure illustrates how religious preference can influence family size.

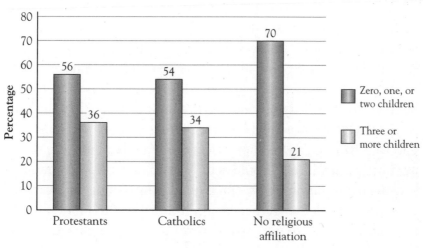

Ideal Family Size by Religious Preference

June 11–14, 2007

SOURCE: Joseph Carroll, "Americans: 2.5 Children Is 'Ideal' Family Size," Gallup, June 26, 2007, www.gallup.com/poll/27973/Americans-25-Children-Ideal-Family-Size.aspx.

Birth Control

Susan and her husband, Damon, both twenty-seven, have one daughter, Rosie, who just turned two. High school sweethearts, they've known each other since first grade and went all through parochial school together. When I asked about their feelings about using birth control, Susan became very animated.

"We grew up Catholic, and we love the church," she said. "But we think about birth control all the time. And it's not just me and Damon—a lot of our friends are struggling with what to do. I've heard that a lot of Catholics think that the church should change its mind about birth control. But it hasn't, and I'm not ready to be that much of a rebel.

"My sister doesn't think about it and she doesn't use anything, and she's got six kids. I love my nieces and nephews dearly, but as for me? I don't know. My friend Elizabeth is on the pill for cramps—she's had unbearable periods ever since she was twelve—and she's feeling like it's for health reasons, so it doesn't go against the church. Right now, Damon and I are practicing something called the Fertility Awareness Method, which is basically trying to understand when you're ovulating and avoiding sex around the times when you're most fertile. That seems like a good compromise to me, at least for now. And so far, so good."

When I asked Zelda and Hersh about their attitudes toward birth control, Zelda told me an interesting story. "My husband heard a well-known rabbi give a speech recently in which he said that if couples would practice more family planning, meaning birth control, they would actually end up with larger families because they wouldn't burn out as quickly by having children that are spaced too close together. Isn't it ironic that this rabbi is implying that it is okay to use birth control toward the greater goal of having larger family sizes?

"And," she continued, "this rabbi did not say to have as many children as possible, but hopefully we'll have a large happy family. For my circle of friends, the average number of children is four to seven. In the Chassidic communities that surround our neighborhood, six to twelve children is the average."

"From my perspective," says Jack, "there was no consideration of how many children we would have; that wasn't even a question. We would get married, be together, and love each other, and however it worked . . . it would work out. We proceeded along with life, and as the children came along, fine, we would just accommodate them. Whatever the Lord sends, that's what will take place, and he will help provide. So that's the way it all worked out."

Intervals Between Children

"When it comes to the intervals between our children," says Ellen, "we call it 'God's Spacing.' We were always open to a child, and we still are today. I nursed each one of my children, and so I wouldn't have a menstrual cycle for a year. We didn't space them. That is the natural law, the natural process. That is the way a woman's body is made. We are open to the gift of another baby now, but at the same time we'd adjust and be okay if it's not going to happen. For our whole marriage, we have been and will continue to be open to life. Menopause is a part of natural law, and it means the sun has set. We will be thankful for what we have been given."

Zelda and Hersh see the interval issue from a different perspective. I asked Zelda whether she was planning more children after she gave birth in September. "I am turning thirty-nine, and we don't want to be having children after I am forty years old," she said. "So I think we won't plan on having more after this baby. We're both very comfortable with where we are, and what we have.

"After our first child, all the others were carefully discussed. We would analyze together: Is this a good time for another baby? How much time should we put between our children? How are the sibling relationships doing?

"Our decisions were directed by open communication and what we each felt that we could handle and what was doable for us at that time. Part of the spacing was our recognition that siblings who are closer in age somehow get closer in life. The further apart siblings are means more work for their relationship."

Joanne said, "We stopped having children for a while after seven—I was really tired."

"It was not predetermined," Jack adds.

"We both agreed that my health was a priority, so we slowed the pace of having children, and then, after number nine, we stopped completely."

Families with Special Needs

The approximately 8.5 million children in the United States with serious physical, emotional, mental, and developmental disorders requiring early intervention, special services, and other supports are considered children with special needs. Being the parent of such a child can bring many surprising gifts, but it can also take an ongoing emotional and physical toll that may change over time but does not let up.

In the past, children with special needs were almost routinely institutionalized. Today, however, thinking has changed. Findings by researchers led by Theresa J. Early at Ohio State University, described in the *Journal of Family Issues*, "give finer shape to an emerging philosophy for treating children with emotional disorders that favors caregiving by the child's family as opposed to foster care or hospital treatment. According to this view, which has been gaining support among researchers and mental healthcare professionals since the 1980s, children with emotional and behavioral challenges do better when cared for at home by their close family, as compared to when they are yanked away to an unfamiliar environment."[16]

Early and her colleagues found, however, that "caring for children with emotional disorders can take a toll on the child's family, causing harm to the family's well-being. The effects tend to worsen over time," which suggests that families and caregivers don't always get used to caring for these children.

When I deliver trainings or seminars, I frequently dedicate them to parents of children with special needs. They are my heroes.

Stress on Marriage

Pearl, thirty-three, is a midwife, and her husband, Randy, thirty-four, is a product designer. They have been married for seven years. Their older son, Paul, is four years old and has cerebral palsy. Their younger son, Henry, is ten months old. They live in St. Louis, Missouri.

"I went into labor with Paul when I was twenty-four weeks pregnant, and the doctors couldn't stop it. I delivered our son that day, and he weighed one-and-a-half pounds. We knew that we would have a long road ahead. For the first days of his life, he was okay, but on the eighth day he became very sick and had a perforated bowel, which was followed by a severe brain bleed. The doctors encouraged us, three, four, five times to take him off life support because his quality of life was uncertain. They said that he would not be able to eat or walk or talk or do anything.

"Up to that point, we never gave any thought to what a child with disabilities needs in life. Randy jumped in and told the doctors, 'No! We're not going to take him off life support, and we want you to do everything that you can for him. This is our child, and we are not going to play God.' Both Randy and I were on the same page—that this is our child, and we will love him regardless. Paul was in the NICU for four months.

"The hospital where Paul was born is where they deliver all of the multiple births in St. Louis. There are many babies there who have very serious conditions. We would meet people where one parent wanted to discontinue life support, and the other one was against doing that. It caused resentment between them. The stress was unbearable. I would hear people say all the time, 'I didn't sign up for this in life.' It is the stress that does them in. If you don't have support, if you don't have time to go out as a couple, or if you don't have a solid marriage to begin with, you will experience big problems. If one spouse wanted the pregnancy, and the other one wasn't ready, and then you add special needs on top of that? It puts a serious strain on a marriage. We saw many divorces of couples who had children in there."

"But our marriage was strong then and even stronger after having our son," says Randy. "When Paul was two years old, he was diagnosed with cerebral palsy, which affects his lower limbs. He talks, and cognitive-wise he is right on track. He walks with a walker. He is one of the greatest things that ever happened to us. He changed us and the way we look at people and accept people. My life is richer because of him. We knew we were given him for a reason, and we accepted his limits. He proves the doctors and their pessimistic predictions wrong on a daily basis."

"I think we've done well," says Kai. His ten-year-old son, Ryan, has multiple disorders. "Having Ryan has even made our marriage stronger in some ways. When we went to couples counseling some time back, with the focus on our son, one issue was how we could get comfortable with leaving our son at home and do activities only with our younger son, Theo. Ryan doesn't travel well, but he and my mom get along great. So with her blessing, and his, we took some vacations alone with Theo. We've done things to have a separate life with him to some extent. It is tough. Our son has sleep issues, and often we are completely exhausted, and that adds to the stress of everyday life. Any type of government assistance can really help. Our state, Ohio, provides good services, such as respite care, but you have to be aggressive in order to get it."

Family Support

Early and her colleagues found that child functioning and caregiver well-being affected each other. "How upset parents are about their own lives affected their child's behavior," Early writes. "And the child's behavior had an effect on the parents' overall well-being."

On the basis of these conclusions, the researchers recommend providing counseling and other kinds of support to families of children with emotional disorders. "It's not just the children with problems who need care, the people caring for them also need help. Our mental health care services need to pay attention to the families of these kids, because the family members are the primary caregivers."[17] "Starting on day one, our families visited Paul in the NICU every single day," says Pearl. "When we finally brought him home from the NICU, they would come over to the house and do his stretches and exercises with him. They still come over and take him to therapy on days when we can't. We also see both sides of our family two to three times each week. They are a huge part of both of our children's lives.

"Family support helped our decision to have another baby. During my second pregnancy, I needed a tremendous amount of help with Paul because I was on bed rest for the majority of my second pregnancy, and couldn't lift him from twelve weeks to thirty-five weeks. We could not have done it without the support of our families.

"Any time we want a night or a weekend to be together and just some quality married couple's time, our parents are here in a flash. My parents just took Paul camping for four days last week. He had so much fun with nature and the outdoors. We take him out to enjoy everything that a typical kid enjoys."

Impact on Siblings

Children with special needs affect the entire family, not just parents. "Some resent the extra demands placed on them at an early age by their disabled siblings, and many feel neglected by their often overburdened parents," says Gretchen Cook. "And many suffer embarrassment about their sibling's inappropriate behavior or abnormal appearance, and they feel guilty about it. . . . Still, many siblings welcome the early maturity and responsibility that comes with having a disabled brother or sister. They are often well-versed in the details of their sibling's disabilities, and they take pride in being able to explain them in sophisticated ways."[18]

Medical Concerns About Having Another Child

"Our seven-year-old son, James, has Angelman syndrome," Felicia told me. "It's a pretty severe disorder, and he will need 24/7 care for his entire life." She spoke matter-of-factly, and I could see she was tired.

Although children with Angelman syndrome are notable for their happy dispositions, they experience a range of serious developmental issues, including minimal speech, inability to walk or balance well, mental retardation, and sleep disorders, which can disrupt the family's patterns. Yet despite these difficulties, Felicia, a journalist, and Ivan, a management consultant, decided to have a second child—a daughter, now five. Felicia explained their thinking:

"A family with special needs is shaped like a triangle," she said. "When you have a child with special needs and that is your only child, all of your focus and energy is on that child, so that the relationship is similar to a triangle with the child being the top point of the triangle. When you have another child, by default, you can no longer focus all of your energy on your child with special needs. So the triangle morphs into a circle, and having another child rounds out your family and makes your family complete. Now that your family is a circle, the love, attention, and focus on your children goes round and round and gets spread equally."

I asked Ivan whether they've thought about having a third child. "The first bridge we had to cross was whether to have a second child," he said. "We always wanted two children. When you have a child with special needs, and it is a genetic disorder, even though not hereditary, you still have an amazing fear when having your second child. You think to yourself, my God, what if we have two children with disabilities?

"We get tons from our first son, James, and he is amazing. But he will never get married, never go to college, never even say our names. But we get all that from our daughter, which is wonderful. There is some rationale for having a third child, in the special needs context. We think a lot about the burden that our daughter will have when we are long gone. Our son will need somebody to be his guardian and protector. It's going to be a tough job for just one person, especially when she gets a family of her own. So we do occasionally think to ourselves, wouldn't it be nice to have an additional typical child?"

Felicia added, "We are looking at our own ages and the entire family picture. In some ways, it would be nice for our daughter to have another sibling, as well as for our son. But another baby would put our already hectic world into a topsy-turvy state—even more so than it is now!"

REALITY CHECK
Planning for the Future of Children with Special Needs

In addition to the age of the child and the severity of the disability, family finances play a significant role in the decision of when or whether to have another baby in a family with special needs. Ivan and Felicia are typical of parents who understand well that their children with disabilities will never be independent, and what that means for the future. "We have been fortunate regarding finances, which is a huge issue for many families with special needs," says Ivan. "Our income and family support, especially from my parents, has eased that burden significantly. To think about lifelong care for a child on top of your own retirement is a considerable burden."

Sue Shellenbarger, in her *Wall Street Journal* column, described how parents of children with special needs need to plan for the future: "Ever since he began talking, Joan White's son, Michael, now 20, who is disabled and unable to read or write, has been begging her regularly for one reassurance: '*Mommy, say you will never die.*' Michael's disabilities, including Cerebral Palsy, retardation, and epilepsy, prevent him from holding a regular job. He can't imagine how he will get along after his mother is gone. Ms. White, aged 56, can't imagine it either. A single mother who lives in Yonkers, New York, she is trying to plan for her son's future. But the cost and complexity are overwhelming. 'I am afraid for Michael,' she admits, 'which is why I have to live forever.'"[19]

Planning for adult care is becoming more and more necessary as medical advances mean that more and more children with

(Continued)

disabilities are going to outlive their parents. "The average life span of a Down's syndrome child, for instance, has doubled to 50 years from 25 in a single generation," Shellenbarger notes.[20] According to researcher Sonja Rasmussen of the U.S. National Center on Birth Defects and Developmental Disabilities, Atlanta, "Almost half of all babies born with the syndrome have congenital heart defects, and many of these are severe. Medical treatments for these defects have improved in recent years. . . . Also, people with the condition may have been institutionalised in the past. Today, most live in group homes or other facilities in the community."[21]

Yet, says Shellenbarger, only about 10 percent to 20 percent of families with disabled children have done much financial planning. Planning for the future and assigning a guardian are crucial steps toward ensuring a life of care for your child after you are gone. Even beginning to think realistically about taking these kinds of active, positive steps can help immensely to lighten what may seem like an overwhelming responsibility.

Adoptive Families

According to national estimates, nearly 1.6 million children under eighteen in the United States live with adoptive parents,[22] and approximately 127,000 children are adopted annually.[23] Adoption is particularly useful for infertile couples who are seeking children. The majority of the 1 percent of women of childbearing age who adopt a child (547,000 women) are doing so as a result of primary or secondary infertility.

Adoption and Family Size Decision Making

Adoption affects all the individuals involved in the adoption triangle: the adopted child, the biological children (if any), and the adoptive parents.

Couples who strongly desire to be parents and have exhausted all efforts at becoming pregnant through natural means and fertility treatments will look to adoption to solve their difficulty. They may choose to adopt one or two children and stop. Or they may adopt a child and at the same time continue to try for a biological child. Sometimes, parents who were unable to conceive before adopting find that they are, indeed, fertile. It happens quite frequently that a biological child is born after her parents have adopted another child.

Adoption is the least difficult scenario for making family size decisions because the typical adoptive family is led by adults who desire to be parents and who calculate and plan each child, one at a time, being mindful of the individual, marital, and parenting concerns. They also control, to a large extent, the spacing. And they value their children dearly.

According to the National Survey of Adoptive Parents, "Parents of adopted children show them lots of attention—they are more likely to be read to every day as young children (68 percent versus 48 percent in the general population). And 87 percent of adopted children have parents who say they would *definitely* make the same decision to adopt their children. Adopted children do well in school. More than half perform at excellent or very good levels in reading and math, according to their parents."[24]

My recommendation to couples who are considering adopting or have already adopted a child is identical to my advice to typical couples who ask, "How many children should we have?" The answer is as many or as few, as long as you think it through. Family size decisions should be no different for adoptive families than typical biological families—although this is one situation where parents naturally and inevitably make many conscious choices as part of what is sometimes a long, difficult, but ultimately rewarding process.

REALITY CHECK
Does Ethnicity Influence Births?

This partial table shows the birth rate for a variety of demographic groups, based on age, ethnicity, and educational level.

| | Total | Margin of error | Women with births in the past 12 months | | | | Percentage of women who had a birth in the past 12 months who were unmarried | Margin of error |
			Number	Margin of error	Rate per 1,000 women	Margin of error		
Women 15 to 50 years	75,860,506	+/–14,624	4,260,731	+/–16,994	56	+/–1	33.5%	+/–0.3
15 to 19 years	10,536,824	+/–11,859	286,007	+/–5,094	27	+/–1	83.5%	+/–0.6
20 to 34 years	29,854,450	+/–11,093	3,141,602	+/–16,640	105	+/–1	33.4%	+/–0.3
35 to 50 years	35,469,232	+/–13,685	833,122	+/–8,639	23	+/–1	16.8%	+/–0.5
RACE AND HISPANIC OR LATINO ORIGIN								
One race	74,385,454	+/–21,269	4,172,623	+/–16,884	56	+/–1	33.2%	+/–0.3
White	54,548,478	+/–22,159	2,906,065	+/–15,523	53	+/–1	26.5%	+/–0.3
Black or African American	10,438,751	+/–12,586	617,906	+/–7,709	59	+/–1	66.7%	+/–0.7
American Indian and Alaska Native	656,804	+/–5,103	47,399	+/–1,992	72	+/–3	57.8%	+/–2.5
Asian	3,823,848	+/–8,070	220,057	+/–4,586	58	+/–1	11.1%	+/–0.5
Native Hawaiian and Other Pacific Islander	131,370	+/–2,374	7,799	+/–1,008	59	+/–8	43.1%	+/–5.9
Some other race	4,786,203	+/–19,342	373.397	+/–6,116	78	+/–1	39.7%	+/–0.8

Two or more races	1,475,052	+/-13,207	88,108	+/-2,913	60	+/-2	45.9%	+/-1.3
Hispanic or Latino origin (of any race)	11,849,620	+/-5,620	896,291	+/-8,820	76	+/-1	37.9%	+/-0.5
White alone, not Hispanic or Latino	48,000,008	+/-9,751	2,418,648	+/-13,411	50	+/-1	24.7%	+/-0.3
CITIZENSHIP STATUS								
Native	64,159,724	+/-33,106	3,406,448	+/-16,403	53	+/-1	36.2%	+/-0.3
Foreign born	11,700,782	+/-32,734	854,283	+/-8,945	73	+/-1	22.6%	+/-0.4
EDUCATIONAL ATTAINMENT								
Less than high school graduate	14,316,848	+/-40,672	757,026	+/-10,147	53	+/-1	54.9%	+/-0.5
High school graduate (includes equivalency)	18,820,236	+/-46,650	1,103,522	+/-10,625	59	+/-1	45.8%	+/-0.5
Some college or associate's degree	23,987,562	+/-38,066	1,242,654	+/-10,747	52	+/-1	33.3%	+/-0.5
Bachelor's degree	13,073,261	+/-38,715	773,351	+/-8,530	59	+/-1	9.0%	+/-0.3
Graduate or professional degree	5,662,599	+/-27,859	384,178	+/-5,957	68	+/-1	6.0%	+/-0.4

SOURCE: Adapted from U.S. Census Bureau, American Community Survey, Table S1301, Fertility (data set: 2006–2008 American Community Survey 3-Year Estimates), http://factfinder.census.gov/servlet/STTable?_bm5y&-geo_id501000US&-qr_name5ACS_2008_3YR_G00_S1301&-ds_name5ACS_2008_3YR_G00_&-_lang5en&-redoLog5false&-format5&-CONTEXT5st.

We Are Family

Mila's family of origin is Russian Jewish. Her husband, Antonio, raised Catholic in Buenos Aires, is of mixed African, Portuguese, and German heritage. In their late twenties, they have two children and identify themselves as a multiracial family. Or, as Antonio puts it, "We're just an American family."

According to the Population Reference Bureau, "Intermarried couples, intermarried families, and multiracial and multiethnic children increasingly populate the American landscape. In some communities, especially in Hawaii and California, it would not be surprising if the average person were to conclude that intermarriage and multiracial and multiethnic children are the norm."[25]

I asked Mila if she thought culture and ethnicity had an influence on their family size, and that of other families she knew.

"I'm an only child, and Antonio comes from a pretty large family. We have three kids because that just seemed right to us. As for our spiritual life, we are sort of finding our own way right now.

"But no matter what religion or race one is," Mila says, "being American and living in the United States and having an American mentality and culture is probably the biggest influence. Catholics aren't supposed to use birth control, but Antonio's sisters do. And my friends from college, who pretty much cover the gamut of race and religion, all waited to start a family until after they finished school and started their careers. You can say that's a stereotype, but I think it just upholds our good old American values to be financially secure and able to provide for a family rather than caving to dogmatic religious or ethnic pressures."

Self-Test
How Do Old (and New) Family Traditions Affect Your Family Size?

Please consider the following statements carefully. If you'd like to use them as a multiple-choice test to get a snapshot of where you stand on various issues we've raised, follow the rating system below. If you'd like to think more deeply about yourself in relation to certain issues, I encourage you to write down your thoughts in a journal.

I also encourage you to consider these statements in concert with your partner. It's a great way to discover how you differ in your attitudes toward children and family, and to find shared areas of agreement that will help make your choices easier.

There are no objective points to add up as you review your responses: your decisions here are subjective. You and your partner will determine the weight of each statement as it pertains to your needs. Feel free to revisit these statements. You may find that over time, your responses will change.

If your responses bring up hidden issues you have never considered, or reveal problem areas in your marriage that need work, I encourage you to seek help. You can find support from family or parenting support groups (run either by peers or by professionals—teachers, counselors, therapists, clergy, or others in the community) or from licensed therapists. Insist that a major focus of the outside support should be the goal of preparing yourself to have a first child or another child, or simply being able to agree, "Our family is complete."

A wise professor of mine once stated, "There are no problems, only projects." If you decide on support or counseling, start soon. Both of your biological clocks are ticking!

Blended Families

My children from my first marriage would welcome another sibling.

STRONGLY AGREE   AGREE   DON'T KNOW   DISAGREE   STRONGLY DISAGREE

We need to have our own child—it will make us a real family.

STRONGLY AGREE   AGREE   DON'T KNOW   DISAGREE   STRONGLY DISAGREE

I'm worried that a new baby will make my children from my first marriage feel left out.

STRONGLY AGREE   AGREE   DON'T KNOW   DISAGREE   STRONGLY DISAGREE

We just got married, second time for both of us, and we can't wait to start a new family! Why wait?

STRONGLY AGREE   AGREE   DON'T KNOW   DISAGREE   STRONGLY DISAGREE

I'm worried about being a stepparent to my partner's children, but maybe having my own child will make a difference.

STRONGLY AGREE   AGREE   DON'T KNOW   DISAGREE   STRONGLY DISAGREE

We're so in love—not like my first marriage. Our own children will make our relationship even stronger.

STRONGLY AGREE   AGREE   DON'T KNOW   DISAGREE   STRONGLY DISAGREE

My ex has custody, so I barely see my children as it is. I'm worried that a new child will give me no time for them at all.

STRONGLY AGREE   AGREE   DON'T KNOW   DISAGREE   STRONGLY DISAGREE

Culture and Religion

I'm not that religious, but my wife says everyone in her family has five or more children, so she wants that many too, or her mom and sisters will think I'm a bad influence.

STRONGLY AGREE   AGREE   DON'T KNOW   DISAGREE   STRONGLY DISAGREE

Our religious faith encourages us to have a large family, but I worry that I won't be able to handle so many children without financial support.

STRONGLY AGREE   AGREE   DON'T KNOW   DISAGREE   STRONGLY DISAGREE

My partner wants to use birth control, but I was raised in a religion that doesn't allow it—the whole idea makes me uncomfortable.

STRONGLY AGREE   AGREE   DON'T KNOW   DISAGREE   STRONGLY DISAGREE

My ultraliberal, ultrapolitical mother thinks we're irresponsible to have more than two children, given world starvation and dwindling human resources all over the planet.

STRONGLY AGREE   AGREE   DON'T KNOW   DISAGREE   STRONGLY DISAGREE

I want to have only girls, since way more men in this family and in our neighborhood wind up in trouble with the law for one reason or another.

STRONGLY AGREE   AGREE   DON'T KNOW   DISAGREE   STRONGLY DISAGREE

Families with Special Needs

We already have one child with special needs. We want another child, but worry that he or she might have special needs, too.

STRONGLY AGREE   AGREE   DON'T KNOW   DISAGREE   STRONGLY DISAGREE

I want to give my child with special needs a brother or sister to help take care of him after we're gone.

STRONGLY AGREE   AGREE   DON'T KNOW   DISAGREE   STRONGLY DISAGREE

We need to have one typical child to get the kind of experiences our child with special needs can't give us.

STRONGLY AGREE   AGREE   DON'T KNOW   DISAGREE   STRONGLY DISAGREE

Epilogue

We began this book by considering a simple but telling question: Why do *you*—not your partner, your parents, or your friends—want to have children? By now, I hope that you and your partner have gained some insight and understanding not only about the *why* of adding children to your family but about *whether* you really want to, and if you do, *when*.

Decisions about the timing, spacing, and number of children in your family are some of the most important ones that you can make. Please, never let yourself be coerced or shamed into having another child. Although there are many issues to consider—including health, career, lifestyle, finances, and deeper issues such as culture and tradition—there is only one basic guideline: you should have as many or as few children as you fervently want—whether that's one or eleven!—provided you and your partner think it through.

A healthy, loving, low-conflict parenting relationship is the heart of your family, the powerhouse that keeps it going strong. I urge you both to value and nurture this relationship for your own sakes and for your children's security and well-being. Think about whether this is the ideal time for your family to grow in size, rather than what is the *ideal family size*.

The best and only reason to have another child is that you both truly love the child you have, you love being parents, and you want another child regardless of its gender. I believe that the question you and your partner should ask—and it needs to be asked each time you consider increasing your family size—is this: "Are we ready to have our first child, or another child, now?"

I hope this book has been, and will be, useful in making choices about each new child in your family, and that I've helped you feel better equipped to make this important decision. I genuinely hope that the insights you have achieved through considering and discussing what you've read here will give you tools that you and your partner can use to create *your* perfect family size.

Self-Tests: Family Size Choice

Here's a summary of all the previous self-tests to do again now that you've read the whole book and thought about what it means for your particular, special, unique family situation. Take your time, do it with your most significant other or others, and put it to good use.

Self-Test
Why Do You Want to Have Children?

Social Pressures

I want to give my parents a grandchild.

STRONGLY AGREE　　AGREE　　DON'T KNOW　　DISAGREE　　STRONGLY DISAGREE

All of my friends have children.

STRONGLY AGREE　　AGREE　　DON'T KNOW　　DISAGREE　　STRONGLY DISAGREE

People tell me it would be "selfish" not to have children.

STRONGLY AGREE　　AGREE　　DON'T KNOW　　DISAGREE　　STRONGLY DISAGREE

I want to give my child a sibling.

STRONGLY AGREE　　AGREE　　DON'T KNOW　　DISAGREE　　STRONGLY DISAGREE

My tradition favors large families—it's our duty to procreate.

STRONGLY AGREE　　AGREE　　DON'T KNOW　　DISAGREE　　STRONGLY DISAGREE

Your Childhood Experiences

My parents were great when I was growing up.

STRONGLY AGREE　　AGREE　　DON'T KNOW　　DISAGREE　　STRONGLY DISAGREE

My parents were terrible role models.

STRONGLY AGREE　　AGREE　　DON'T KNOW　　DISAGREE　　STRONGLY DISAGREE

I'm close to my siblings.

STRONGLY AGREE　　AGREE　　DON'T KNOW　　DISAGREE　　STRONGLY DISAGREE

I have poor relationships with my siblings.

STRONGLY AGREE　　AGREE　　DON'T KNOW　　DISAGREE　　STRONGLY DISAGREE

Expectations: Myth Versus Reality

A child will be a great distraction from my own issues.

STRONGLY AGREE　　AGREE　　DON'T KNOW　　DISAGREE　　STRONGLY DISAGREE

I don't want to be lonely later in life.

STRONGLY AGREE　　AGREE　　DON'T KNOW　　DISAGREE　　STRONGLY DISAGREE

My child will be my best friend.

STRONGLY AGREE　　AGREE　　DON'T KNOW　　DISAGREE　　STRONGLY DISAGREE

My child will be like me and have my values.

STRONGLY AGREE　　AGREE　　DON'T KNOW　　DISAGREE　　STRONGLY DISAGREE

My child will accomplish what I never achieved.

STRONGLY AGREE   AGREE   DON'T KNOW   DISAGREE   STRONGLY DISAGREE

It will be fun to have children!

STRONGLY AGREE   AGREE   DON'T KNOW   DISAGREE   STRONGLY DISAGREE

I don't think I can handle one more child.

STRONGLY AGREE   AGREE   DON'T KNOW   DISAGREE   STRONGLY DISAGREE

Self-Test
When Is the Best Time for You to Have Children?

Your Age Now—and Later

I'm too young to have children—I'm not even twenty.

STRONGLY AGREE   AGREE   DON'T KNOW   DISAGREE   STRONGLY DISAGREE

I'm in my twenties, and I'm ready to start a family now.

STRONGLY AGREE   AGREE   DON'T KNOW   DISAGREE   STRONGLY DISAGREE

I'm in my twenties, and I'm tired all the time.

STRONGLY AGREE   AGREE   DON'T KNOW   DISAGREE   STRONGLY DISAGREE

I'm only in my thirties—I've got a few more years before I have to worry about fertility.

STRONGLY AGREE   AGREE   DON'T KNOW   DISAGREE   STRONGLY DISAGREE

I'm over forty—I don't think I can even get pregnant at my age.

STRONGLY AGREE   AGREE   DON'T KNOW   DISAGREE   STRONGLY DISAGREE

I'm too old to have children—I don't want to be mistaken for my child's grandparent!

STRONGLY AGREE   AGREE   DON'T KNOW   DISAGREE   STRONGLY DISAGREE

Your Job Versus Your Career

I'm really busy at work; it's hard to get enough time for my family as it is.

STRONGLY AGREE   AGREE   DON'T KNOW   DISAGREE   STRONGLY DISAGREE

We both plan to take time off work to bond with the new baby.

STRONGLY AGREE   AGREE   DON'T KNOW   DISAGREE   STRONGLY DISAGREE

I'm thinking about giving up my job and being a stay-at-home parent.

STRONGLY AGREE   AGREE   DON'T KNOW   DISAGREE   STRONGLY DISAGREE

We'll both work at home.

STRONGLY AGREE   AGREE   DON'T KNOW   DISAGREE   STRONGLY DISAGREE

We'll both go back to work, and the children will be in day care all day or with a babysitter.

STRONGLY AGREE   AGREE   DON'T KNOW   DISAGREE   STRONGLY DISAGREE

I'm not sure we're earning enough to afford another child.

STRONGLY AGREE   AGREE   DON'T KNOW   DISAGREE   STRONGLY DISAGREE

Your Relationship

We need time together as a couple before we have children.

STRONGLY AGREE   AGREE   DON'T KNOW   DISAGREE   STRONGLY DISAGREE

My children are my first priority—my partner needs to understand that.

STRONGLY AGREE   AGREE   DON'T KNOW   DISAGREE   STRONGLY DISAGREE

Physical and Emotional Health

I've been healthier . . . but I'm sure I'd feel better if I were pregnant.

STRONGLY AGREE   AGREE   DON'T KNOW   DISAGREE   STRONGLY DISAGREE

My last pregnancy was so difficult that I wonder if I can go through that again.

STRONGLY AGREE   AGREE   DON'T KNOW   DISAGREE   STRONGLY DISAGREE

I'm afraid of postpartum depression.

STRONGLY AGREE   AGREE   DON'T KNOW   DISAGREE   STRONGLY DISAGREE

I don't know if I can handle raising another child—I'm already exhausted.

STRONGLY AGREE   AGREE   DON'T KNOW   DISAGREE   STRONGLY DISAGREE

How Far Apart?

I just want to get it over with—why be pregnant for years and years?

STRONGLY AGREE   AGREE   DON'T KNOW   DISAGREE   STRONGLY DISAGREE

My own siblings were perfectly spaced, and I want to replicate that.

STRONGLY AGREE   AGREE   DON'T KNOW   DISAGREE   STRONGLY DISAGREE

We want one more, but I don't know what we'll do if it's twins!

STRONGLY AGREE   AGREE   DON'T KNOW   DISAGREE   STRONGLY DISAGREE

Self-Test
How Many Children Can Your Relationship Hold?

The Relationship Factor

I already work too hard around the house. Another child will add to my load.

STRONGLY AGREE   AGREE   DON'T KNOW   DISAGREE   STRONGLY DISAGREE

I think I share in chores and child rearing, but my partner disagrees.

STRONGLY AGREE   AGREE   DON'T KNOW   DISAGREE   STRONGLY DISAGREE

The idea of a relationship-centered family rather than a child-centered family makes me uncomfortable.

STRONGLY AGREE   AGREE   DON'T KNOW   DISAGREE   STRONGLY DISAGREE

Be Partners, Not Adversaries

We argue about how to raise our children all the time, but we're thinking about having more.

STRONGLY AGREE   AGREE   DON'T KNOW   DISAGREE   STRONGLY DISAGREE

A child (or another child) will make our marriage stronger.

STRONGLY AGREE   AGREE   DON'T KNOW   DISAGREE   STRONGLY DISAGREE

Having a child (or another child) will make us happier.

STRONGLY AGREE   AGREE   DON'T KNOW   DISAGREE   STRONGLY DISAGREE

Having a child (or another child) will put a wedge between us.

STRONGLY AGREE   AGREE   DON'T KNOW   DISAGREE   STRONGLY DISAGREE

Learning from Experience

I'm still recovering my body and energy from my last pregnancy—I can't be romantic and take care of another child too.

STRONGLY AGREE   AGREE   DON'T KNOW   DISAGREE   STRONGLY DISAGREE

Our children are so big now   I miss having babies.

STRONGLY AGREE   AGREE   DON'T KNOW   DISAGREE   STRONGLY DISAGREE

Our relationship is so solid now that the children are older. We can handle another child.

STRONGLY AGREE   AGREE   DON'T KNOW   DISAGREE   STRONGLY DISAGREE

Self-Test

Small, Moderate, Large . . . What's Your Ideal Family Size?

One-Child Families

Only children are lonely.

STRONGLY AGREE   AGREE   DON'T KNOW   DISAGREE   STRONGLY DISAGREE

Only children are spoiled.

STRONGLY AGREE   AGREE   DON'T KNOW   DISAGREE   STRONGLY DISAGREE

Depriving my child of siblings would be cruel.

STRONGLY AGREE   AGREE   DON'T KNOW   DISAGREE   STRONGLY DISAGREE

Only children get high-quality attention from parents.

STRONGLY AGREE   AGREE   DON'T KNOW   DISAGREE   STRONGLY DISAGREE

I'm an only child, and I would not want my child to grow up alone.

STRONGLY AGREE   AGREE   DON'T KNOW   DISAGREE   STRONGLY DISAGREE

I'm an only child, and I miss the support of someone who "knows my story."

STRONGLY AGREE   AGREE   DON'T KNOW   DISAGREE   STRONGLY DISAGREE

I was unhappy with my siblings, and I don't want my child to go through that.

STRONGLY AGREE   AGREE   DON'T KNOW   DISAGREE   STRONGLY DISAGREE

I don't want my child to have to take care of me all alone when I get old.

STRONGLY AGREE   AGREE   DON'T KNOW   DISAGREE   STRONGLY DISAGREE

It's not fair to raise a child in a family of adults.

STRONGLY AGREE   AGREE   DON'T KNOW   DISAGREE   STRONGLY DISAGREE

My pregnancy was difficult, and I just don't want to go through that again.

STRONGLY AGREE   AGREE   DON'T KNOW   DISAGREE   STRONGLY DISAGREE

Two Children

Two is the perfect number of children to have.

STRONGLY AGREE   AGREE   DON'T KNOW   DISAGREE   STRONGLY DISAGREE

Two children are perfect—one for each parent.

STRONGLY AGREE   AGREE   DON'T KNOW   DISAGREE   STRONGLY DISAGREE

Everyone I know has two children.

STRONGLY AGREE   AGREE   DON'T KNOW   DISAGREE   STRONGLY DISAGREE

Friends and family are pressuring us to give our child siblings.

STRONGLY AGREE   AGREE   DON'T KNOW   DISAGREE   STRONGLY DISAGREE

Our careers won't allow us to have a larger family.

STRONGLY AGREE   AGREE   DON'T KNOW   DISAGREE   STRONGLY DISAGREE

Three or Four Children
Small families are better.

STRONGLY AGREE   AGREE   DON'T KNOW   DISAGREE   STRONGLY DISAGREE

Large families are better.

STRONGLY AGREE   AGREE   DON'T KNOW   DISAGREE   STRONGLY DISAGREE

I can't handle any more children than we already have.

STRONGLY AGREE   AGREE   DON'T KNOW   DISAGREE   STRONGLY DISAGREE

I don't feel like I'm done having children.

STRONGLY AGREE   AGREE   DON'T KNOW   DISAGREE   STRONGLY DISAGREE

My partner wants a larger family, but I don't.

STRONGLY AGREE   AGREE   DON'T KNOW   DISAGREE   STRONGLY DISAGREE

I've always wanted more children, but my partner is happy with what we have.

STRONGLY AGREE   AGREE   DON'T KNOW   DISAGREE   STRONGLY DISAGREE

It's bad for the environment to keep adding people.

STRONGLY AGREE   AGREE   DON'T KNOW   DISAGREE   STRONGLY DISAGREE

More children would make our home chaotic—I need some quiet time.

STRONGLY AGREE   AGREE   DON'T KNOW   DISAGREE   STRONGLY DISAGREE

More children would make our home happy—I don't mind the noise.

STRONGLY AGREE   AGREE   DON'T KNOW   DISAGREE   STRONGLY DISAGREE

We just want to try one more time to see if we can get a boy (or girl).

STRONGLY AGREE   AGREE   DON'T KNOW   DISAGREE   STRONGLY DISAGREE

We really can't afford to have more children than we already have.

STRONGLY AGREE   AGREE   DON'T KNOW   DISAGREE   STRONGLY DISAGREE

We really want more children, and we can find a way to afford them.

STRONGLY AGREE   AGREE   DON'T KNOW   DISAGREE   STRONGLY DISAGREE

Large Families
Large families are great—they have more love than small families.

STRONGLY AGREE   AGREE   DON'T KNOW   DISAGREE   STRONGLY DISAGREE

Children get lost in a large family.

STRONGLY AGREE   AGREE   DON'T KNOW   DISAGREE   STRONGLY DISAGREE

More children would mean one of us would have to be a stay-at-home parent, and neither of us wants to do that.

STRONGLY AGREE   AGREE   DON'T KNOW   DISAGREE   STRONGLY DISAGREE

Self-Test
How Do Old (and New) Family Traditions
Affect Your Family Size?

Blended Families

My children from my first marriage would welcome another brother or sister.

STRONGLY AGREE   AGREE   DON'T KNOW   DISAGREE   STRONGLY DISAGREE

We need to have our own child—it will make us a real family.

STRONGLY AGREE   AGREE   DON'T KNOW   DISAGREE   STRONGLY DISAGREE

I'm worried that a new baby will make my children from my first marriage feel left out.

STRONGLY AGREE   AGREE   DON'T KNOW   DISAGREE   STRONGLY DISAGREE

We just got married, second time for both of us, and we can't wait to start a new family! Why wait?

STRONGLY AGREE   AGREE   DON'T KNOW   DISAGREE   STRONGLY DISAGREE

I'm worried about being a stepparent to my partner's children, but maybe having my own child will make a difference.

STRONGLY AGREE   AGREE   DON'T KNOW   DISAGREE   STRONGLY DISAGREE

We're so in love—not like my first marriage. Our own children will make our relationship even stronger.

STRONGLY AGREE   AGREE   DON'T KNOW   DISAGREE   STRONGLY DISAGREE

My ex has custody, so I barely see my children as it is. I'm worried that a new child will give me no time for them at all.

STRONGLY AGREE   AGREE   DON'T KNOW   DISAGREE   STRONGLY DISAGREE

Culture and Religion

I'm not that religious, but my wife says everyone in her family has five or more children, so she wants that many too, or her mom and sisters will think I'm a bad influence.

STRONGLY AGREE   AGREE   DON'T KNOW   DISAGREE   STRONGLY DISAGREE

Our religious faith encourages us to have a large family, but I worry that I won't be able to handle so many children without financial support.

STRONGLY AGREE   AGREE   DON'T KNOW   DISAGREE   STRONGLY DISAGREE

My partner wants to use birth control, but I was raised in a religion that doesn't allow it—the whole idea makes me uncomfortable.

STRONGLY AGREE   AGREE   DON'T KNOW   DISAGREE   STRONGLY DISAGREE

Old and New Traditions

My ultraliberal, ultrapolitical mother thinks we're irresponsible to have more than two children, given world starvation and dwindling human resources all over the planet.

STRONGLY AGREE   AGREE   DON'T KNOW   DISAGREE   STRONGLY DISAGREE

I want to have only girls, since way more men in this family and in our neighborhood wind up in trouble with the law for one reason or another.

STRONGLY AGREE   AGREE   DON'T KNOW   DISAGREE   STRONGLY DISAGREE

Families with Special Needs

We already have one child with special needs. We want another child, but worry that he or she might have special needs, too.

STRONGLY AGREE   AGREE   DON'T KNOW   DISAGREE   STRONGLY DISAGREE

I want to give my child with special needs a brother or sister to help take care of him after we're gone.

STRONGLY AGREE   AGREE   DON'T KNOW   DISAGREE   STRONGLY DISAGREE

We need to have one typical child to get the kind of experiences our child with special needs can't give us.

STRONGLY AGREE   AGREE   DON'T KNOW   DISAGREE   STRONGLY DISAGREE

Notes

Chapter 1: Why Do You Want to Have Children?

1. Anna Quindlen, *Loud and Clear* (New York: Random House, 2004), 58.

2. Sue Shellenbarger, "Cost of Raising a Child Ticks Up," *Wall Street Journal* blog, June 10, 2010, http://blogs.wsj.com/juggle/2010/06/10/cost-of-raising-a-child-ticks-up/. For complete information and a Cost of Raising a Child Calculator, read the USDA's current annual report at www.cnpp.usda.gov/ExpendituresonChildrenbyFamilies.htm.

3. Lois Wladis Hoffman and Jean Denby Manis, "The Value of Children in the United States: A New Approach to the Study of Fertility," *Journal of Marriage and Family* 41 (August 1979): 583–596.

4. Lisa Belkin, "Does Having Children Make You Unhappy?" Motherlode: Adventures in Parenting, *New York Times* (online edition), April 1, 2009, http://parenting.blogs.nytimes.com/2009/04/01/why-does-anyone-have-children/.

Chapter 2: When Is the Best Time for You to Have Children?

1. LiveStrong.com, "Teen Pregnancy," www.livestrong.com/article/12457-teen-pregnancy/.
2. American Society for Reproductive Medicine, "Age and Fertility" (Patient Information Series), 2003, www.ASRM.org.
3. The miscarriage rate (34 percent) is triple for women between forty and forty-four, compared to those ages twenty to twenty-nine (10 percent). The risk of having a child with Down syndrome increases from 1 in 1,250 for a twenty-five-year-old mother, to 1 in 30 for a forty-five-year-old mother. American Society for Reproductive Medicine, "Age and Fertility: A Guide for Patients," 2003, www.asrm.org/publications/detail.aspx?id=2507.
4. Craig Kliger, "Too Old to Be a Mom? The Issues," *Good Housekeeping*, September 29, 2000, www.goodhousekeeping.com/family/new-moms/too-old-mom-0900.
5. "Fast Facts About Infertility," Resolve.org, February 28, 2008, www.resolve.org/about/fast-facts-about-fertility.html.
6. American Society for Reproductive Medicine, "Age and Fertility."
7. Antonia Abbey, Frank M. Andrews, and L. Jill Halman, "Infertility and Subjective Well-Being: The Mediating Roles of Self-Esteem, Internal Control, and Interpersonal Conflict," *Journal of Marriage and Family*, May 1992, 408–417.
8. "One cycle of IVF costs an average of $12,400. The cost for GIFT ranges from $8,000 to $13,000." American College of Obstetricians and Gynecologists, *Women's Health Stats and Facts: 2007 Pocket Guide*, 20. "Revenues from fertility treatment jumped from $41,000,000 in 1986 to nearly $3,000,000,000 in 2002." Barbara Dafoe Whitehead, "Where Is Technological Reproduction Taking Us?" *Commonweal* 133, no. 18 (October 20, 2006).
9. U.S. Census Bureau, "America's Families and Living Arrangements: 2007," September 2009, www.census.gov/population/www/socdemo/hh-fam/p20-561.pdf.

10. M. P. Dunleavy, Uncommon Sense, "Cost of Being a Stay-at-Home Mom: $1 Million," MSN.com, http://articles .moneycentral.msn.com/CollegeAndFamily/RaiseKids/ CostOfBeingAStayAtHomeMom.aspx.

11. American Academy of Pediatrics, Parenting Corner Q&A: Working Mothers, www.aap.org/publiced/bk0_workingmoth- ers.htm.

12. Lyneka Little, "How Stay-at-Home Dads Bounce Back from Career Hiatus," ABC News/Money, October 28, 2010, http://abcnews.go.com/Business/role-reversal-unemployment- creates-stay-home-fathers/story?id=11983642.

13. Richard Fry and D'Vera Cohn, "Women, Men and the New Economics of Marriage" (January 19, 2010), quoted in Bruce Sallan, "A Dad's Point-of-View," AtHomeDad.org, posted July 6, 2010, www.athomedad.org/.

14. Wendy Bonovich, "Parenting/AOL/Mom Debate," *Parenting*, November 2006.

15. William Doherty, *Take Back Your Marriage* (New York: Gilford Press, 2001), 60.

16. The maternal death rate in the United States, which just ninety years ago was one in every one hundred live births, was only thirteen per hundred thousand in 2004. "More U.S. Women Dying in Childbirth," MSNBC.com, Pregnancy, www.msnbc.msn.com/id/20427256/.

17. Ellen Galinsky, *Ask the Children* (New York: Morrow, 1999), 62.

18. P. Ramchandani and others, "Paternal Depression in the Postnatal Period and Child Development: A Prospective Population Study," *Lancet* 365 (2005): 2201–2205, cited in Norman Swan, "Postnatal Depression in Fathers," Health Minutes, ABC Health &Wellbeing, August 25, 2008, www. abc.net.au/health/minutes/stories/2005/08/25/1445891.htm.

19. Bao-Ping Zhu, Robert T. Rolfs, Barry E. Nangel, and John M. Horan, "Effect of the Interval Between Pregnancies on Perinatal Outcomes," *New England Journal of Medicine* 340 (February 25, 1999): 589–594. The medical researchers

analyzed data from 173,205 infants born in Utah between 1989 and 1996.

20. Helen Fisher, *Anatomy of Love* (New York: Fawcett Columbine, 1992), 299.

21. Sarah Ebner, "What Is the Perfect Age Gap Between Children?" *The Times*, January 17, 2009, http://women.time-sonline.co.uk.

22. Zhu, Rolfs, Nangel, and Horan, "Effect of the Interval."

23. Meridian Group International, "Reproductive Health: Birth Spacing and Family Planning," www.meridian-group.com/birth_spacing.html.

24. Between 1990 and 2004, multiple births climbed an average of 3 percent annually for a total increase of 42 percent since 1990, and 70 percent since 1980. Joyce A. Martin and others, "Births: Final Data for 2005," *National Vital Statistics Reports* 56, no. 6 (December 5, 2007), www.cdc.gov/nchs/data/nvsr/nvsr56/nvsr56_06.pdf.

25. Nick Collins, "Parents of Twins 'More Likely to Divorce,'" *Telegraph*, March 16, 2010, www.telegraph.co.uk/science/science-news/7452522/Parents-of-twins-more-likely-to-divorce.html.

Chapter 3: How Many Children Can Your Relationship Hold?

1. William Doherty, *Take Back Your Marriage* (New York: Gilford Press, 2001), 60.

2. "What Makes a Marriage Work?" (chart), in Pew Research Center, *As Marriage and Parenthood Drift Apart, Public Is Concerned About Social Impact* (July 1, 2007), http://pewsocialtrends.org/files/2010/10/Marriage.pdf.

3. Jay Belsky and John Kelly, *The Transition to Parenthood* (New York: Delacorte Press, 1994), 124.

4. Stephanie Coontz, "Till Children Do Us Part," *New York Times*, February 5, 2009, www.nytimes.com/2009/02/05/opinion/05iht-edcoontz.1.19959819.html?scp=3&sq=Till%20Children%20Do%20Us%20Part&st=cse.

5. John Gottman, *Why Marriages Succeed or Fail* (New York: Simon & Schuster, 1994), 157–158.

6. Ellen Galinsky, *Ask the Children* (New York: Morrow, 1999), 151.

7. Gottman, *Why Marriages Succeed or Fail*, 157–158.

8. Elaine D. Eaker, Lisa M. Sullivan, and Margaret Kelly-Hayes, "Marital Status, Marital Strain, and the Risk of Coronary Heart Diseases on Total Mortality: The Framingham Offspring Study," *Psychosomatic Medicine* 69 (2007): 509–513.

9. Carolyn Pape Cowan and Philip A. Cowan, *When Partners Become Parents* (Mahwah, NJ: Erlbaum, 1992), 206.

10. Ibid., 10.

11. Coontz, "Till Children Do Us Part."

12. Belsky and Kelly, *The Transition to Parenthood*, 16.

13. Norval Glenn and Sarah McLanahan, "Children and Marital Happiness: A Further Specification of the Relationship," *Journal of Marriage and Family*, February 1982, 63–72.

14. Lynn White, Alan Booth, and John Edwards, "Children and Marital Happiness, Why the Negative Correlation?" *Journal of Family Issues* 7, no. 2 (June 1986): 131–147.

15. Linda Lyons, "Oh, Boy: Americans Still Prefer Sons," Gallup Organization, September 23, 2003.

16. Richard Morin, "The Boy Bias," *Washington Post*, February 8, 2004, B5.

17. Cowan and Cowan, *When Partners Become Parents*, 156.

18. Tim B. Heaton, "Marital Stability Throughout the Child-Rearing Years," *Demography* 27, no. 1 (February 1990): 55–63.

19. Ayelet Waldman, "Truly, Madly, Guiltily," *New York Times*, March 27, 2005, www.nytimes.com/2005/03/27/fashion/27love.html?pagewanted2&sq Truly, Madly, Guiltily&stcse&scp1.

20. Doherty, *Take Back Your Marriage*, 48, 51, 57, 60.

Chapter 4: Small, Moderate, Large . . . What's Your Ideal Family Size?

1. Lisa Belkin, "How Many Children Is Too Many?" Motherlode: Adventures in Parenting, *New York Times*

Magazine, September 2, 2010, http://parenting.blogs.nytimes
.com/2009/02/09/how-many-children-is-too-many/.
2. Pew Research Center, "The New Demography of American
Motherhood," revised August 19, 2010, http://pewsocialtrends
.org/files/2010/10/754-new-demography-of-motherhood.pdf.
(The following figure appears on p. 18.)

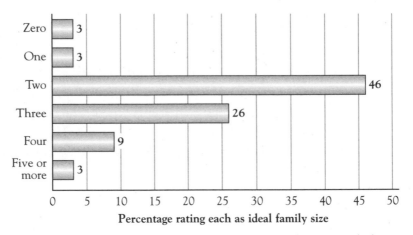

Most Americans Want Two or Three Children

Note: "Don't know/refused" responses not shown. Respondents were asked:
"What is the ideal number of children for a family to have?"

3. Lauren Sandler, "The Only Child: Debunking the Myths,"
Time, July 8, 2010, www.time.com/time/nation/article/
0,8599,2002382-1,00.html.
4. Lauren Sandler, "The Only Child Myth," *Time*, July 8, 2010,
www.time.com/time/nation/article/0,8599,2002382,00.html.
5. Denise Polit and Toni Falbo, "Only Children and Personality
Development: A Quantitative Review," *Journal of Marriage
and Family* 49 (May 1987): 309–325.
6. Tina Kelley, "Company for an Only Child, and for
Parents, Peace of Mind," *New York Times*, June 3,
2007, www.nytimes.com/2007/06/03/nyregion/03only

.html?scp=1&sq=Company%20for%20an%20Only%20
Child,%20and%20for%20Parents,%20Peace%20of%20
Mind&st=cse.

7. Nancy Hass, "We Are Family, Mom, Dad, and Just
Me," *New York Times*, October 24, 1999, www.nytimes
.com/1999/10/24/style/we-are-family-mom-dad-and-just-me
.html?scp=1&sq=We%20Are%20Family,%20Mom,%20
Dad,%20and%20Just%20Me&st=cse.

8. Joseph Rogers, PhD, a professor of psychology at the University
of Oklahoma in Norman, who evaluated the IQs of about eight
thousand children, says, "Many factors, including genetics, are
more influential in a child's intelligence. Even those who argue
that family size affects a child's intelligence and academic performance concede that parents' income and education levels
may matter more." Quoted in Deborah Pike Olsen, "Is a Bigger
Family Better?" *Child*, September 2006, 145–150.

9. Joseph E. Rodgers, H. Harrington Cleveland, Edwin van den
Oord, and David Rowe, "Resolving the Debate Over Birth
Order, Family Size, and Intelligence," *American Psychologist*,
June 2000, 599–612. Another supportive boost for this
approach to the data comes from James Higgins. "In a separate
study of IQ, James V. Higgins of Michigan State University
in East Lansing reports that larger families correlate with
lower IQs among children. In his analysis of 300 families,
Higgins reports that parents of large families tended to have
lower IQs, and concludes that children, therefore, inherited
similar IQ levels. Conversely, he says, those parents with
higher IQs tended to produce children with higher IQs." In
Jay Greenberg, "Family Size Tied to SAT IQ Scores," *Science
News* 127, no. 22 (June 1, 1985): 340.

10. Anne Cassidy, *Parents Who Think Too Much* (New York: Dell,
1998), 260.

11. Pamela Paul, "Three Kids? You Showoffs," *Washington Post*,
April 6, 2008, www.washingtonpost.com/wp-dyn/content/
article/2008/04/04/AR2008040403217.html.

12. Jennifer Eyre White, "Having Three Kids," www.havingthreekids .com/surveys.html.

13. Jennifer Eyre White, "An Interview with Dr. Heidi Murley," www.havingthreekids.com/murleyinterview.html.

14. Jennifer Nelson, "More Than Two?" SFGate, Commentary, March 7, 2004, www.sfgate.com/cgi-bin/article.cgi?file=/ c/a/2004/03/07/cmgod54v3k6.dtl&type=printable.

15. Bill McKibben, *Maybe One* (New York: Penguin Group, 1998).

16. Ben J. Wattenberg, *The Birth Dearth* (New York: Pharos Books, 1987), 129.

17. Mary Ann Glendon and Mary Haynes, "Putting Fertility First," *New York Times*, October 20, 1999.

18. Kate Zernike, "And Baby Makes How Many?" *New York Times*, February 8, 2009, www.nytimes.com/2009/02/08/ fashion/08bigfam.html?scp=1&sq=And+Baby+Makes+H ow+Many%3F&st=nyt.

19. Ibid.

20. David Adamson, Nancy Belden, Julie Devonzo, and Sally Patterson, *How Americans View World Population Issues* (Santa Monica, CA: RAND, 2000), 39–40.

21. Luchina Fisher, "Like the Duggars: Growing Up in Large Families Is Mixed Blessing," ABC News/Entertainment, September 4, 2009, http://abcnews.go.com/Entertainment/ Television/growing-duggar-size-families-mixed-blessing/ story?id=8485349.

22. Quoted in Deborah Pike Olsen, "Is a Bigger Family Better?" *Child*, September 2006, 145–150.

Chapter 5: How Do Old (and New) Family Traditions Affect Your Family Size?

1. Pew Research Center, "The New Demography of American Motherhood," revised August 19, 2010, http://pewsocialtrends .org/files/2010/10/754-new-demography-of-motherhood.pdf. (Data cited appears on pp. 3, 8, 1.)

2. Henry J. Kaiser Family Foundation, "Race, Ethnicity & Health Care" (July 2006), www.kff.org/minorityhealth/upload/7541.pdf.

3. National Healthy Marriage Resource Center, "Native Americans," www.healthymarriageinfo.org/marriage-and-culture/native-americans#NA.

4. Sally C. Clarke, "Advance Report of Final Divorce Statistics, 1989 and 1990," *Monthly Vital Statistics Report* 43, no. 9, supplement (March 22, 1995). Final data from the Centers for Disease Control and Prevention and the National Center for Health Statistics.

5. Ibid.

6. Susan D. Stewart, "How the Birth of a Child Affects Involvement with Stepchildren, *Journal of Marriage and Family* 67 (May 2005): 464–473.

7. Linda Little, "Children of Same-Sex Couples Do as Well as Other Children," Medscape Today, www.medscape.com/viewarticle/514477.

8. Susan Donaldson James, "'Gayby Boom' Fueled by Same-Sex Parents," ABC News/Health, August 3, 2009, http://abcnews.go.com/Health/ReproductiveHealth/story?id=8232392&page=1.

9. Mackenzie Carpenter, "What Happens to Kids Raised by Gay Parents?" *Pittsburgh Post-Gazette*, June 10, 2007, www.post-gazette.com/pg/07161/793042-51.stm.

10. Alice Park, "Study: Children of Lesbians May Do Better Than Their Peers," *Time*, June 7, 2010, www.time.com/time/health/article/0,8599,1994480,00.html#ixzz0z9OAWNhW.

11. Goldscheider and Mosher (1991) and Lehrer (1996), cited in Alicia Adsera, "Religion and Changes in Family-Size Norms in Developed Countries," *Review of Religious Research* 47, no. 3 (2006): 271–286.

12. Heaton (1986), Mosher and others (1992), and Lehrer (1996), cited in Adsera, "Religion and Changes," 272.

13. Mosher and others (1992) and Lehrer (1996), cited in Adsera, "Religion and Changes," 272.

14. Pew Forum on Religion & Public Life, U.S. Religious Landscape Survey, "Reports," http://religions.pewforum.org/reports.

15. Joseph Carroll, "Americans: 2.5 Children Is 'Ideal' Family Size," Gallup News Service, June 26, 2007, www.gallup.com/poll/27973/americans-25-children-ideal-family-size.aspx.

16. Theresa J. Early, Thomas K. Gregoire, and Thomas P. MacDonald, "Child Functioning and Caregiver Well-Being, in Families of Children with Emotional Disorders: A Longitudinal Analysis," *Journal of Family Issues* 23 (2002): 374–391.

17. Ibid.

18. Gretchen Cook, "Siblings of Disabled Have Their Own Troubles," *New York Times*, April 4, 2006, www.nytimes.com/2006/04/04/health/04sibs.html.

19. Sue Shellenbarger, "Lessons in Letting Go: How Parents of Disabled Children Plan for the Future," *Wall Street Journal*, May 29, 2003, www.sternco.com/pdf/MerrillLynch/ML_SpecialNeedsTrust_WallStreetJournal_29May03.pdf.

20. Ibid.

21. Quoted in Emma Young, "Down's Syndrome Lifespan Doubles," *New Scientist*, March 22, 2002, www.newscientist.com/article/dn2073-downs-syndrome-lifespan-doubles.html.

22. Rose M. Kreider, "Number of Children of Householder by Type of Relationship and Age: 2000" (Table 1), *Adopted Children and Step-Children 2000* (Washington, DC: U.S. Census Bureau, October 2003).

23. National Adoption Information Clearing House, *How Many Children Were Adopted in 2000 and 2001?—Highlights*, August 2004.

24. Sharon Vandivere, Karen Malm, and Laura Radel, *Adoption U.S.A.: A Chart Book Based on the 2007 National Survey of Adoptive Parents* (Washington, DC: U.S. Department of Health and Human Services, Office of the Assistant Secretary for Planning and Evaluation, 2009).

25. Sharon M. Lee and Barry Edmonston, "New Marriages, New Families: U.S. Racial and Hispanic Intermarriage," *Population Bulletin* 60, no. 2 (2005): 33, www.prb.org/pdf05/60.2newmarriages.pdf.

Selected Resources

Although there are many fine books, blogs, organizations, and popular films and television shows about parenting and families, the most valuable resource I can recommend for determining whether this is the right time to add a child to your family is still—above all—you and your partner's well-considered thoughts on the matter. Nevertheless, there are resources that can stimulate your thinking and inspire your own creative ideas for addressing your unique situation.

The Internet is a great way to find all kinds of family and parenting resources right where you live. If you do a general online search on "parents networks," you will find that many communities across the United States have online local parents' listings that recommend everything from child care, schools, and classes to housing, financial, and medical resources; kids' activities; shopping, gardening, and painting resources; and much more. Search on the term "parents network" and add the name of your community to find the one that's best for you. You can also look at bulletin boards at your food market, maternity shops, and toys stores; check out day-care centers and preschool classes; and ask your friends who have kids.

Here are some other resources, all of which you need to consider for yourself and judge if they're helpful to you and your special family dynamic.

Family Finances

If you would like to learn more about the cost of raising a family, the USDA's Cost of Raising a Child Calculator (www.cnpp .usda.gov/calculatorintro.htm) can help you estimate the yearly cost of raising a child up to the age of eighteen, customized for your family and your region of the United States. It takes into consideration housing, food, transportation, clothing, health care, child care, and miscellaneous expenses, and will give you good insight into the realities of raising a family in America today.

BabyCenter.com's First-Year Baby Costs Calculator (www.babycenter.com/babyCostCalculator.htm) helps you estimate how much your baby's first year of life might cost, based on your own needs and intentions. Your input and results give you a very good idea of areas where you can reduce costs immediately. (Do you really need that $600 stroller, or would the $100 basic model give you more to spend on food and diapers?)

Parenting and Families

Discover the resources you have right in your local community. If you are looking for hands-on activities like local workshops, training, classes, or support groups for parents, check your local newspapers, children's stores, bulletin boards, school sources, or pediatrician's office for listings. Online, use your local parents network.

Dr. Bill Doherty's Web site (www.drbilldoherty.org/) is for parents, couples, educators, therapists, journalists, community organizers, and others. You'll find resources on parenting, marriage, and couples therapy.

MSNBC's Parenting Web site (http://today.msnbc.msn.com/id/3041445/) has current articles and videos on everything from parenting advice to slashing your grocery bill.

Lisa Belkin's *New York Times* blog Motherlode: Adventures in Parenting (http://parenting.blogs.nytimes.com/) is a rich resource for discussion of a range of parenting issues—"homework, friends, sex, baby sitters, eating habits, work-family balance and so much more"—and Belkin actively invites readers to share their diverse experiences.

BabyCenter.com (www.babycenter.com) has a wide variety of resources for parents of, well, babies, and is an especially good source of free online cost calculators and calendaring, listing, and planning tools for pregnancy, birth, travel, and other baby-year needs.

If you live in a city, check out the UrbanBaby.com (www.UrbanBaby.com) "lively message boards section, where parents come day and night to share, discuss and ask questions related to parenting and their lives as parents. [It] is a place for honest, uninhibited discussions, quick answers, banter and community."

There are, of course, a variety of periodicals catering to families and parents, and I urge you to explore these at your local bookstore or magazine stand. You can also find a number of magazines online. Parenting.com (www.Parenting.com) is the online home of two magazines, *Parenting* and *BabyTalk*, and features articles from both sources as well as reader interaction. You can read *Parents* magazine online at www.parents.com/.

Finally, if you'd like to learn more about my thoughts on families and marriage, I invite you to visit my blog, (www.FamilyThinking.com), or follow me on Twitter (http://twitter.com/dralansinger).

Relationships

You can find help for your relationship in the same way that you might look for sources of parenting support: check the Internet for local support groups, and look at bulletin boards in such community gathering places as supermarkets, the YMCA, schools, and religious institutions for notices regarding support groups and peer-led group meetings. You can also find support and therapy groups that are led by professionals—teachers, psychotherapists, social workers, and religious leaders.

If you and your partner feel you might benefit from couples counseling, I encourage you to try it. Look for a licensed therapist in your area—he or she may be a social worker, marriage and family counselor, psychologist, or psychiatrist—with whom both you and your partner feel comfortable. Don't be afraid to speak to more than one therapist before choosing the one you feel is the best fit for your beliefs and goals. Your family doctor, local health center, or trusted friends may all be good sources for referrals.

The National Registry of Marriage Friendly Therapists (www.marriagefriendlytherapists.com/), cofounded by Dr. Bill Doherty, lists qualified therapists throughout the United States "who value marriage and lifelong commitment."

Smart Marriages: The Coalition for Marriage, Family, and Couples Education (http://smartmarriages.com/index.html) "is dedicated to making marriage education widely available—to getting the information couples need to create successful marriages out of the research labs and clinical offices and to the public." It's a good site for information that's user-friendly, affordable, and accessible.

The Gottman Relationship Institute (www.gottman.com/) "applies leading-edge research on marriage in a practical, down-to-earth therapy and trains therapists committed to helping couples." The institute has books, DVDs, and workshops for couples, and information about couples therapy.

Divorce Busting (www.divorcebusting.com/), the Web site of best-selling author and marriage therapist Michele Weiner-Davis, MSW, specializes in "helping people stop divorce and get their marriage back on track." Find information about talking to a marriage sex coach or telephone coach, or schedule a private marriage counseling session.

Data Related to Families and Children

The Internet has an abundance of good research on families and children and associated topics. The following selection is not exhaustive, nor is it meant to be definitive. I do hope it will give you a good start if you are interested in exploring these issues on a more academic level.

Miscellaneous

- Centers for Disease Control (www.cdc.gov/)
- MedLine Plus (www.nlm.nih.gov/medlineplus/sitemap.html)
- Pew Research Center (http://pewresearch.org/)
- Public Agenda (www.publicagenda.org/)

Marriage

- Institute for Marriage and Public Policy (www.marriagedebate .com/index.php)
- The National Marriage Project (www.virginia.edu/ marriageproject/)
- PREP, Inc., Divorce Prevention and Marriage Enhancement Program (www.prepinc.com)

Families and Parenting

- Families and Work (www.familiesandwork.org/)
- University of New Hampshire, Sociology Research Laboratory, Papers on Children and Parenting (http://pubpages .unh.edu/~mas2/#Papersavailable)

Children

- American Academy of Pediatrics (www.aap.org/advocacy/ mmarticles.htm)
- Child Trends (www.childtrends.org/)

- National Institute of Child Health and Human Development (www.nichd.nih.gov/)
- Kids Count Data Center (http://datacenter.kidscount.org/Default.aspx)
- Kids Risk (www.kidsrisk.org/index.html)
- Society for Research in Child Development (www.srcd.org/)

Bibliography

Adamson, David, Nancy Belden, Julie Devonzo, and Sally Patterson. *How Americans View World Population Issues*. Santa Monica: RAND, 2000.

Barnett, Rosalind C., and Caryl Rivers. *She Works, He Works*. Cambridge, MA: Harvard University Press, 1996.

Barry, Dave. *Dave Barry's Guide to Marriage and/or Sex*. New York: Rodale, 1987.

Belkin, Lisa. *Life's Work*. New York: Simon & Schuster, 2002.

Belsky, Jay, and John Kelly. *The Transition to Parenthood*. New York: Delacorte Press, 1994.

Berggraf, Shirley. *The Feminine Economy and Economic Man*. Reading, MA: Addison-Wesley, 1997.

Blake, Judith. "The Only Child in America: Prejudice Versus Performance." *Population and Development Review*, March 1981, 7(1), 43–54.

———. "Family Size and Quality of Children." *Demography*, November 1981, 18(4), 421–442.

Bonovich, Wendy. "Parenting/AOL-Mom Debate." *Parenting*, November 2006.

Borba, Michele. *The Big Book of Parenting Solutions*. San Francisco: Jossey-Bass, 2009.

Bronson, Po, and Ashley Merryman. "Will This Marriage Last?" *Time*, June 30, 2006. www.time.com/time/nation/article/0,8599,1209784,00.html.

Brooks, David. "The Power of Marriage." *New York Times*, November 22, 2003. www.nytimes.com/2003/11/22/opinion/the-power-of-marriage.html?scp=1&sq=The%20Power%20of%20Marriage&st=cse.

Brooks, Robert, and Sam Goldstein. *Raising Resilient Children*. Lincolnwood, IL: Contemporary Books, 2001.

Bryant, Vaughn. "Kissing—a Research Paper." Unpublished study, Texas A&M University, October 29, 2006.

Buss, David. "God (or Not), Physics and, of Course, Love: Scientists Take a Leap." *New York Times*, January 4, 2005. www.nytimes.com/2005/01/04/science/04edgehed.html?_r=1&scp=1&sq=David%20Buss%20January%204,%202005&st=cse.

Carey, Benedict. "Holding Loved One's Hand Can Calm Jittery Neurons." *New York Times*, January 31, 2006. www.nytimes.com/2006/01/31/health/psychology/31marr.html?scp=2&sq=Holding+Loved+One%92s+Hand+Can+Calm+Jittery+Neurons&st=nyt.

Carnegie, Dale. *How to Win Friends and Influence People*. New York: Simon & Schuster, 1936.

Cassidy, Anne. *Parents Who Think Too Much*. New York: Dell, 1998.

Chapman, Gary. *The Five Love Languages*. Chicago: Northfield, 1992.

Cockrell, Stacie, Cathy O'Neill, and Julia Stone. *Babyproofing Your Marriage*. New York: HarperCollins, 2007.

Cohen, Robert Stephen. *Reconcilable Differences*. New York: Atria Books, 2002.

Cool, Lisa Collier. "Am I Normal?" *Good Housekeeping*, March 2001, 73.

Coontz, Stephanie. *Marriage, a History: From Obedience to Intimacy, or How Love Conquered Marriage*. New York: Penguin Books, 2005.

———. "How Love Conquered Marriage." Lecture, Psychotherapy Networker Symposium, March 2006.

———. "Till Children Do Us Part." *New York Times*, February 5, 2009. www.nytimes.com/2009/02/05/opinion/05iht-edcoontz.1.19959819.html?scp=3&sq=Till%20Children%20Do%20Us%20Part&st=cse.

Cosby, Bill. *Fatherhood*. New York: Berkley Books, 1986.

Cowan, Carolyn Pape, and Philip A. Cowan. *When Partners Become Parents*. Mahwah, NJ: Erlbaum, 1992.

Crittenden, Ann. *The Price of Motherhood*. New York: Henry Holt, 2001.

Damon, William. *Greater Expectations*. New York: Simon & Schuster, 1995.

Deveny, Kathleen. "We're Not in the Mood." *Newsweek*, June 30, 2003. www.newsweek.com/2003/06/29/we-re-not-in-the-mood.html.

Dobson, James D. *The New Dare to Discipline*. Wheaton, IL: Tyndale House, 1992.

Doherty, William. "In the Community." Plenary, Smart Marriages conference, July 1999.

———. "Nurturing Intentional Marriage." Paper presented at the Smart Marriages conference, July 1999.

———. *Take Back Your Kids*. Notre Dame, IN: Sorin Books, 2000.

———. "Take Back Your Marriage." Paper presented at the Smart Marriages conference, July 2001.

———. *Take Back Your Marriage*. New York: Gilford Press, 2001.

———. "To Leave or Stay? Couples on the Brink." Lecture at the Psychotherapy Networker Symposium, March 2004.

———. "Marriage-Friendly Therapy." Paper presented at the Smart Marriages conference, July 2005.

Doherty, William, and Barbara Carlson. *Putting Family First*. New York: Henry Holt, 2002.

Downey, Douglas B. "When Bigger Is Not Better: Family Size, Parental Resources, and Children's Educational Performance." *American Sociological Review*, October 1995, 60, 746–761.

Eaker, Elaine D., Lisa M. Sullivan, and Margaret Kelly-Hayes. "Marital Status, Marital Strain, and the Risk of Coronary Heart Disease or Total Mortality: The Framingham Offspring Study." *Psychosomatic Medicine*, 2007, 69, 509–513. www.psychosomat icmedicine.org/cgi/content/abstract/69/6/509.

Edmondson, Brad. "From Birth to Battle." *American Demographics*, May 1991.

Elias, Maurice, Steven Tobius, and Brian Friedlander. *Emotionally Intelligent Parenting*. New York: Random House, 1999.

Fisher, Helen. *Anatomy of Love*. New York: Fawcett Columbine, 1992.

Flowers, Blaine J. *Beyond the Myth of Marital Happiness*. San Francisco: Jossey-Bass, 2000.

Galinsky, Ellen. *Ask the Children*. New York: Morrow, 1999.

Gellman, Marc. "A Voyage Apart in the Same Direction." *Newsweek*, June 2, 2005. http://lists101.his.com/pipermail/ smartmarriages/2005-June/002748.html.

Georgia, Jennifer. [Letter to the editor regarding Kathleen Deveny's June 30, 2003, article]. *Newsweek*, July 14, 2003.

Gigy, Lynn, and Joan B. Kelly. "Reasons for Divorce: Perspectives of Divorcing Men and Women." *Journal of Divorce and Remarriage*, 1992, *18*(1/2), 174–175.

Gladwell, Malcolm. *Blink*. New York: Little, Brown, 2005.

Glenn, Norval, and Sarah McLanahan. "Children and Marital Happiness: A Further Specification of the Relationship." *Journal of Marriage and Family*, February 1982, pp. 63–72.

Gookin, Sandra. *Parenting for Dummies*. New York: Hungry Minds, 2002.

Gottman, John. *Why Marriages Succeed or Fail*. New York: Simon & Schuster, 1994.

———. Plenary, Smart Marriages conference, July 1998.

———. *The Seven Principles for Making Marriage Work*. New York: Three Rivers Press, 1999.

———. *The Relationship Cure*. New York: Crown, 2001.

———. "And Baby Makes Three." Lecture, Smart Marriages conference, July 2004.

Gottman, John, and Julie Schwartz Gottman. *And Baby Makes Three*. New York: Random House, 2007.

Gray, John. *Men Are from Mars, Women Are from Venus*. New York: HarperCollins, 1992.

Greenberg, Jay. "Family Size Tied to SAT IQ Scores." *Science News*, June 1, 1985, *127*(22), 340.

Grundfest, Bill, and Janet Grundfest. "Married and Clueless." *Olam*, Summer 2002.

Hallowell, Edward, and Michael Thompson. *Finding the Heart of the Child*. Braintree, MA: Association of Independent Schools in New England, 1993.

Harley, Willard F. *His Needs, Her Needs*. Grand Rapids, MI: Revell, 1986.

Hass, Nancy. "We Are Family: Mom, Dad, and Just Me." *New York Times*, October 24, 1999. www.nytimes.com/1999/10/24/style/we-are-family-mom-dad-and-just-me.html?scp=1&sq=We%20Are%20Family,%20Mom,%20Dad,%20and%20Just%20Me&st=cse.

Heaton, Tim B. "Marital Stability Throughout the Child-Rearing Years." *Demography*, February 1990, *27*(1), 55.

Hewlett, Sylvia Ann. *Creating a Life*. New York: Talk Miramax Books, 2002.

Heymann, Jody. *The Widening Gap*. New York: Basic Books, 2000.

Hoffman, Lois Wadis, and M. Hoffman. "The Value of Children to Parents." In N.J.T. Fawcett, Ed., *Psychological Perspectives on Population* (pp. 106–151). New York: Basic Books, 1973.

Institute for American Values. *Why Marriage Matters: Twenty-One Conclusions from the Social Sciences*. Pamphlet. New York: Institute for American Values, 2002.

Jordan, Pamela L., Scott M. Stanley, and Howard J. Markman. *Becoming Parents*. San Francisco: Jossey-Bass, 1999.

Kelley, Tina. "Company for an Only Child, and for Parents, Peace of Mind." *New York Times*, June 3, 2007. www.nytimes .com/2007/06/03/nyregion/03only.html?scp=1&sq= Company%20for%20an%20Only%20Child,%20and%20for% 20Parents,%20Peace%20of%20Mind&st=cse.

Kindlon, Dan. *Too Much of a Good Thing*. New York: Hyperion, 2001.

Krasnow, Iris. *Surrendering to Marriage*. New York: Talk Miramax Books, 2002.

Larson, Jeffrey H. *The Great Marriage Tune-Up Book*. San Francisco: Jossey-Bass, 2003.

Latava, Charlotte. "Life with Your First Child and Beyond." *Parenting*, September 2004.

Leach, Penelope. *Children First*. New York: Knopf, 1994.

Leavitt, Steven, and Stephen Dubner. *Freakonomics*. New York: HarperCollins, 2005.

Leonhardt, David. "It's a Girl! (Will the Economy Suffer?)" *New York Times*, October 26, 2003. www.nytimes.com/ 2003/10/26/business/it-s-a-girl-will-the-economy-suffer .html?scp=1&sq=It%92s%20a%20Girl!%20(Will%20 the%20Economy%20Suffer?)&st=cse.

Luo, Shanhong, and Eva C. Klohnen. "Assortative Mating and Marital Quality in Newlyweds: A Couple-Centered Approach." *Journal of Personality and Social Psychology*, 2005, 88(2), 304–326.

———. "Do Opposites Attract, or Do Birds of a Feather Flock Together?" Press release. *Newswise*, February 9, 2005.

Lyons, Linda. "Oh, Boy: Americans Still Prefer Sons." Gallup Organization, September 23, 2003.

Markman, Howard J., Scott M. Stanley, and Susan M. Blumberg. *Fighting for Your Marriage, Third Revised Edition*. San Francisco: Jossey-Bass, 2010.

Marquardt, Elizabeth. *Between Two Worlds*. New York: Crown, 2005.

McKibben, Bill. *Maybe One*. New York: Penguin Group, 1998.

———. "What Only-Child Syndrome?" *New York Times*, May 3, 1998. www.nytimes.com/1998/05/03/magazine/what-only-child-syndrome.html?scp=3&sq=What%20Only-Child%20Syndrome?&st=cse.

McKinney, Maggie. "Return to the Future." *Newsweek*, March 6, 1995.

Morin, Richard. "The Boy Bias." *Washington Post*, February 8, 2004, B5.

Newport, Frank. "Americans Generally Happy with Their Marriages." *Gallup Poll Monthly*, September 1996, p. 19.

Olsen, Deborah Pike. "Is a Bigger Family Better?" *Child*, September 2006, 145–150.

Ornish, Dean. "Love Is Real Medicine." *Newsweek*, October 3, 2005. www.newsweek.com/2005/10/02/love-is-real-medicine.html.

Page, Susan. *Why Talking Is Not Enough*. San Francisco: Jossey-Bass, 2006.

Parker-Pope, Tara. "Marital Spats, Taken to Heart." *New York Times*, October 2, 2007. www.nytimes.com/2007/10/02/health/02well.html?scp=1&sq=Marital%20Spats,%20Taken%20to%20Heart&st=cse.

Pemplin, Noreen. "Parenting/AOL-Mom Debate," *Parenting*, November 2006.

Peterson, Karen S. "Starter Marriage: A New Term for Early Divorce." *USA Today*, January 29, 2002. www.usatoday.com/news/health/2002-01-28-starter-marriage.htm.

———. "Forgiveness Could Be Balm for the Body Too." *USA Today*, October 23, 2003, D08.

Pew Research Center. "The New Demography of American Motherhood," revised August 19, 2010. http://pewsocialtrends.org/files/2010/10/754-new-demography-of-motherhood.pdf.

Pittman, Frank. *Grow Up*. New York: St. Martin's Griffin, 1998.

———. "Marriage-Busting." Smart Marriages conference, July 1999.

———. "Turning Points of Marriage." Psychotherapy Networker conference, March 2005.

———. "Learning from Experience: The Therapist's Life Cycle." Lecture, Psychotherapy Networker Symposium West, March 2006.

Polit, Denise, and Toni Falbo. "Only Children and Personality Development: A Quantitative Review." *Journal of Marriage and Family*, May 1987.

Popenoe, David. "New Day Dawning? In the Struggle over the Family, Foundations Made the Difference." *Philanthropy*, March/April 2002.

Postman, Neil. *The Disappearance of Childhood*. New York: Vintage Books, 1994.

Putnam, Robert. *Bowling Alone*. New York: Simon & Schuster, 2000.

Robinson, John P., and Geoffrey Godbey. *Time for Life*. University Park: Pennsylvania State University Press, 1997.

Rodgers, Joseph Lee, H. Harrington Cleveland, Edwin van den Oord, and David Rowe. "Resolving the Debate over Birth Order, Family Size, and Intelligence." *American Psychologist*, June 2000, pp. 599–612.

Rosenblatt, Paul C. "Behavior in Public Places: Comparison of Couples Accompanied and Unaccompanied by Children." *Journal of Marriage and Family*, November 1974, p. 750.

Ross, Katherine, and Marika Van Willigen. "Gender, Parenthood and Anger." *Journal of Marriage and Family*, August 1996, p. 572.

Rotenberg, Herman, with Melinda Ligos. "With This Ring I Allay Anxiety." *New York Times*, April 4, 2001. http://select.nytimes.com/gst/abstract.html?res=F30A1FFB3D5A0C778CDDAD0894D9404482&scp=4&sq=With%20This%20Ring%20I%20Allay%20Anxiety&st=cse.

Sandler, Lauren. "The Only Child Myth." *Time*, July 19, 2010.

Schlessinger, Laura. *Parenthood by Proxy*. New York: HarperCollins, 2000.

Shapiro, Alyson Fearnley, John M. Gottman, and Sybil Carrere. "The Baby and the Marriage: Identifying Factors That Buffer Against Decline in Marital Satisfaction After the First Baby Arrives." *Journal of Family Psychology*, 2000, *14*(1), 59–70.

Sherman, James. "For a Happy Marriage, Treat Hubby Like Fido." *Newsweek*, November 8, 2004. www.newsweek.com/2004/11/07/for-a-happy-marriage-treat-hubby-like-fido.html.

Simring, Steven, and Sue Klavans Simring. *Making Marriage Work for Dummies*. New York: IDG Books Worldwide, 1999.

Steinberg, Laurence. *Ten Basic Principles of Good Parenting*. New York: Simon & Schuster, 2004.

Steinem, Gloria, and John Bradshaw. "Love." *Psychology Today*, March/April 1993.

Strauss, Alix. *The Joy of Funerals: A Novel in Stories*. New York: St. Martin's Press, 2004, pp. 155–272.

Taffel, Ron. *Nurturing Good Children Now*. New York: St. Martin's Press, 1999.

Tierney, John. "Valentine's Day Homework." *New York Times*, February 14, 2006. http://query.nytimes.com/gst/fullpage.html?res=9C07E5D8123EF937A25751C0A9609C8B63&sec=&spon=&&scp=2&sq=Valentine%E2%80%99s%20Day%20Homework&st=cse.

Touchton, Nicole. "Parenting/AOL-Mom Debate." *Parenting*, November 2006.

Waite, Linda J., and Maggie Gallagher. *The Case for Marriage*. New York: Doubleday, 2000.

Waite, Linda J., and Evelyn L. Lehrer. "The Benefits from Marriage and Religion in the United States: A Comparative Analysis." *Population and Development Review*, June 2003, *29*(2), 255–275.

Waldman, Ayelet. "Truly, Madly, Guiltily." *New York Times*, March 27, 2005. www.nytimes.com/2005/03/27/fashion/27love.html?pagewanted=2&sq=Truly, Madly, Guiltily&st=cse&scp=1.

Wallerstein, Judith. *The Unexpected Legacy of Divorce*. New York: Hyperion Books, 2000.

Warner, Judith. "I Love Them, I Love Him Not." *New York Times*, February 14, 2005. www.nytimes.com/2005/02/14/opinion/14warner.html?scp=1&sq=I+Love+Them%2C+I+Love+Him+Not&st=nyt.

Weiner-Davis, Michele. *Divorce Busting*. New York: Simon & Schuster, 1992.

———. "Divorce Busting." Lecture, Smart Marriages conference, July 1999.

———. *The Divorce Remedy*. New York: Simon & Schuster, 2001.

———. "Forgiveness Is a Gift You Give Yourself." www.Divorce-Busting.com, 2002.

———. "Time Together." www.DivorceBusting.com, 2002.

———. "Guerilla Divorce-Busting Dos and Don'ts." Lecture, Smart Marriages conference, July 2003.

———. "Divorce-Busting Makeover." Lecture, Smart Marriages conference, July 2004.

———. "Divorce-Busting Programs." Lecture, Smart Marriages conference, July 2005.

———. "It Takes One to Tango." Lecture, Psychotherapy Networker conference, March 2006.

White, Lynn, Alan Booth, and John Edwards. "Children and Marital Happiness: Why the Negative Correlation?" *Journal of Family Issues*, June 1986, 7(2), 131.

Zernike, Kate. "And Baby Makes How Many?" *New York Times*, February 8, 2009. www.nytimes.com/2009/02/08/fashion/08bigfam.html?scp=1&sq=And+Baby+Makes+How+Many%3F&st=nyt.

About the Author

Dr. Alan Singer is a marriage and family therapist in private practice since 1978. He provides individual and group therapy at family service agencies and parenting workshops at community centers. He lectures on marriages that thrive, ideal family size, and New Age parenting. Married for thirty-three years, he and his wife, a nurse, live in New Jersey and are the parents of four grown children. He has thirty years of experience as a father.

Singer received his master's degree in social work from Wurzweiler School of Social Work in 1978 and his PhD in social policy and administration from Rutgers University in 1995. He received the Rutgers Graduate School award for his unique research on family size. He has conducted numerous broadcast and print interviews for various media outlets, including *USA Today*, *Fox Morning News*, MSNBC.com, and the *Huffington Post*.

Singer's marriage and family column appears in New Jersey's *Home News Tribune* (www.thnt.com), a sister newspaper of *USA Today*. Singer created the Web site www.FamilyThinking.com, where his columns, television interviews, and podcasts appear. He has a sizeable following on http://twitter.com/dralansinger. In addition, he has been published in the *Jerusalem Post* and is a frequent contributor to the Web site www.SmartMarriages.com.

Index

Down syndrome, 27, 122
Dunleavy, M. P., 34

E
Early, Theresa J., 116
Educational attainment, 125
Emotional health: importance of, 39;
   postpartum depression and, 40;
   psychological nesting and, 42; Self-
   Test on, 49, 136; sleep issues and,
   40–41. *See also* Physical health
Environmental politics, 87
Ethnic families: ethnicity influence
   on birth rates, 124–126;
   "The New Demography of
   Motherhood" report on, 98; social
   and economic pressures on, 99.
   See also Multiracial/multiethnic
   families
Expectations (myth versus reality):
   child's gender as disappointment,
   13; distraction from your adult
   problems, 14–15; fear of handling
   more than one child, 17–18; to
   fulfill your own unfulfilled dreams,
   16–17; to give yourself a best
   friend, 15–16; it will be fun to
   have children, 17; as protection
   from being lonely later, 15; to
   replicate yourself, 16; Self-Test on,
   21, 133–134; understanding your,
   12–14; you've already made your
   plan, 18

F
Falbo, Toni, 74
Families: adoptive, 122–123;
   blended, 97, 100–109, 127–128;
   cost of raising a child for each,
   6–7; ethnicity of, 98–99, 124–126;

gay and lesbian parents, 106–107;
   multiracial and multiethnic, 109,
   126; with special needs children,
   116–122, 128, 142; success not
   dependent on number of children,
   92–93
Families with special needs: impact
   on siblings, 119; importance
   of family support for, 118–119;
   medical concerns about having
   another child, 119–121; planning
   for the future of children with
   special needs, 121–122; research
   on challenges facing, 116; Self-
   Test on, 128, 142; stress on
   marriage in, 117–118
Family of origin: impulse to replicate
   birth spacing of, 45; only children
   of parent from large, 76–77; only
   children of parent from single-
   child, 75–76; your childhood
   experiences in, 11–12, 20
Family size: adoptive families and,
   122–123; blended families and,
   97, 100–109, 127–128; children's
   intelligence and, 80–81; cultural
   and religious factors in, 110–116;
   environmental politics and, 87;
   family as family no matter what
   the size, 92–93; how culture and
   religion affect, 98–99, 110–116;
   how ethnicity influence, 98–99,
   124–126; large, 88–92, 96, 140;
   life with your first, second, and
   third child, 72–73; one-child,
   73–81, 94, 139; Self-Test on,
   93–96, 139–140; three or four
   children, 84–86, 95–96, 140;
   two-child, 81–84, 95, 139–140.
   See also "Ideal" family size

for the future of, 121–122; stress on marriage by, 117–118
Sports, unfulfilled dreams, 17
Spouses. *See* Your relationship
Stay-at-home dads, 34
Stay-at-home parents: career and financial issues of, 34–35; statistics on, 33; of three- or four-child families, 86
Stepfamilies. *See* Blended families
Stewart, Susan D., 106
Stone, Elizabeth, 232
Stress: of children leading to divorce, 53–54; special needs children and marital, 117–118. *See also* Financial stress; Worries
Support systems: children with special needs and, 118–119; large families as, 90–91
Surveys on the Ideal Number of Children (1936–2009), 71

T
Teenage parenthood, 25–26
Third child family life, 72–73
Thirties and parenthood, 27
Three- or four-child families: difference between two children and, 85–86; issues of, 84–85; looking for gender balance driving, 85; Self-Test on, 95–96, 140; stay-at-home parents and, 86. *See also* Large families
Timing of children: career, job, and financial issues, 30–37; financial stability and, 36–37; issues to consider for, 23–24; The Parenting Stages in Years chart on, 24, 25; physical and emotional health, 38–42; possibility of

multiples, 47; Self-Test on, 47–49; waiting until things are "just right," 46; your age now and later, 24–30; your relationship with your partner, 37–38. *See also* Birth spacing
Twenties and parenthood, 26–27
Twins: difficult relationship between, 77; possibility of multiple births, 47
Two-child families: as being a manageable number, 83; difficult pregnancies as reason for stopping, 82; one child for each parent in, 84; perceived as the norm, 81–82; Self-Test on, 95, 139–140; so they will have each other, 82; social pressure factor of, 10, 83–84

U
Unfulfilled dreams, 16–17
U.S. Census Bureau: "America's Families and Living Arrangements: 2007," 33; on gay and lesbian families, 106
U.S. Department of Agriculture, 7
"The U.S. Longitudinal Lesbian Family Study: Psychological Adjustment of 17-Year-Old Adolescents" (Gartrell and Bos), 107
U.S. National Center on Birth Defects and Developmental Disabilities, 122
U.S. Religious Landscape Survey (2007), 111

V
van den Oord, Edwin, 81
The View (TV show), 66